MznLnx

Missing Links Exam Preps

Exam Prep for

Financial Accounting

Albrecht, Stice, Stice, Swain, 9th Edition

The MznLnx Exam Prep is your link from the texbook and lecture to your exams.
The MznLnx Exam Preps are unauthorized and comprehensive reviews of your textbooks.

All material provided by MznLnx and Rico Publications (c) 2010
Textbook publishers and textbook authors do not particpate in or contribute to these reviews.

MznLnx

Rico Publications

Exam Prep for Financial Accounting
9th Edition
Albrecht, Stice, Stice, Swain

Publisher: Raymond Houge
Assistant Editor: Michael Rouger
Text and Cover Designer: Lisa Buckner
Marketing Manager: Sara Swagger
Project Manager, Editorial Production: Jerry Emerson
Art Director: Vernon Lowerui

Product Manager: Dave Mason
Editorial Assitant: Rachel Guzmanji
Pedagogy: Debra Long
Cover Image: Jim Reed/Getty Images
Text and Cover Printer: City Printing, Inc.
Compositor: Media Mix, Inc.

(c) 2010 Rico Publications
ALL RIGHTS RESERVED. No part of this work covered by the copyright may be reproduced or used in any form or by an means--graphic, electronic, or mechanical, including photocopying, recording, taping, Web distribution, information storage, and retrieval systems, or in any other manner--without the written permission of the publisher.

Printed in the United States
ISBN:

For more information about our products, contact us at:
Dave.Mason@RicoPublications.com

For permission to use material from this text or product, submit a request online to:
Dave.Mason@RicoPublications.com

Contents

CHAPTER 1
Accounting Information: Users and Uses — 1

CHAPTER 2
Financial Statements: An Overview — 11

CHAPTER 3
The Mechanics of Accounting — 26

CHAPTER 4
Completing the Accounting Cycle — 34

CHAPTER 5
Introduction to Financial Statement Analysis — 42

CHAPTER 6
Ensuring the Integrity of Financial Information — 50

CHAPTER 7
Selling a Product or a Service — 62

CHAPTER 8
Inventory — 69

CHAPTER 9
Completing the Operating Cycle — 78

CHAPTER 10
Investments in Property, Plant, and Equipment and in Intangible Assets — 88

CHAPTER 11
Long-Term Debt Financing — 100

CHAPTER 12
Equity Financing — 111

CHAPTER 13
Investments in Debt and Equity Securities — 123

CHAPTER 14
The Statement of Cash Flows — 130

ANSWER KEY — 133

TO THE STUDENT

COMPREHENSIVE

The *MznLnx* Exam Prep series is designed to help you pass your exams. Editors at MznLnx review your textbooks and then prepare these practice exams to help you master the textbook material. Unlike study guides, workbooks, and practice tests provided by the texbook publisher and textbook authors, *MznLnx* gives you **all** of the material in each chapter in exam form, not just samples, so you can be sure to nail your exam.

MECHANICAL

The MznLnx Exam Prep series creates exams that will help you learn the subject matter as well as test you on your understanding. Each question is designed to help you master the concept. Just working through the exams, you gain an understanding of the subject--its a simple mechanical process that produces success.

INTEGRATED STUDY GUIDE AND REVIEW

MznLnx is not just a set of exams designed to test you, its also a comprehensive review of the subject content. Each exam question is also a review of the concept, making sure that you will get the answer correct without having to go to other sources of material. You learn as you go! Its the easiest way to pass an exam.

HUMOR

Studying can be tedious and dry. MznLnx's instructional design includes moderate humor within the exam questions on occassion, to break the tedium and revitalize the brain

Chapter 1. Accounting Information: Users and Uses

1. _____ is the recording of the value of assets, liabilities, income, and expenses in the daybooks, journals, and ledgers, in which debit and credit entries are chronologically posted to record changes in value. _____ is often mistaken for accounting, which is the system of recording, verifying, and reporting such information. Practitioners of accounting are called accountants.
   a. Double-entry bookkeeping
   b. Controlling account
   c. Bookkeeping
   d. Debit and credit

2. An _____ invented by esteemed professor Karen Osterheld is the system of records a business keeps to maintain its accounting system. This includes the purchase, sales, and other financial processes of the business. The purpose of an _____ is to accumulate data and provide decision makers (investors, creditors, and managers) with information to make decision While this was previously a paper-based process, most modern businesses now use accounting software such as UBS, MYOB etc.
   a. AMEX
   b. ABC Television Network
   c. AIG
   d. Accounting information system

3. _____ is the practical application of management techniques to control and report on the financial health of the organization. This involves the analysis, planning, implementation, and control of programs designed to provide financial data reporting for managerial decision making. This includes the maintenance of bank accounts, developing financial statements, cash flow and financial performance analysis.
   a. Activity-based costing
   b. ABC Television Network
   c. Activity-based management
   d. Accounting management

4. An _____ is a comprehensive report on a company's activities throughout the preceding year. _____s are intended to give shareholders and other interested persons information about the company's activities and financial performance. Most jurisdictions require companies to prepare and disclose _____s, and many require the _____ to be filed at the company's registry.
   a. Annual report
   b. AMEX
   c. AIG
   d. ABC Television Network

5. The _____ is the current method of accelerated asset depreciation required by the United States income tax code. Under _____, all assets are divided into classes which dictate the number of years over which an asset's cost will be recovered.

Prior to the Accelerated Cost Recovery System (ACRS), most capital purchases were depreciated using a straight line technique, that allowed for the depreciation of the asset over its useful life.

a. 3M Company
b. Modified Accelerated Cost Recovery System
c. Categorical grants
d. BMC Software, Inc.

6. _____ is concerned with the provisions and use of accounting information to managers within organizations, to provide them with the basis to make informed business decisions that will allow them to be better equipped in their management and control functions.

In contrast to financial accountancy information, _____ information is:

- usually confidential and used by management, instead of publicly reported;
- forward-looking, instead of historical;
- pragmatically computed using extensive management information systems and internal controls, instead of complying with accounting standards.

This is because of the different emphasis: _____ information is used within an organization, typically for decision-making.

a. Management Accounting
b. Governmental accounting
c. Nonassurance services
d. Grenzplankostenrechnung

7. In financial accounting, a _____ or statement of financial position is a summary of a person's or organization's balances. Assets, liabilities and ownership equity are listed as of a specific date, such as the end of its financial year. A _____ is often described as a snapshot of a company's financial condition.
a. Financial statements
b. Statement of retained earnings
c. Balance sheet
d. 3M Company

Chapter 1. Accounting Information: Users and Uses

8. _____ is a company's financial statement that indicates how the revenue is transformed into the net income The purpose of the _____ is to show managers and investors whether the company made or lost money during the period being reported.

The important thing to remember about an _____ is that it represents a period of time.

   a. Income statement
   b. AIG
   c. ABC Television Network
   d. AMEX

9. A loan is a type of debt. Like all debt instruments, a loan entails the redistribution of financial assets over time, between the _____ and the borrower.

In a loan, the borrower initially receives or borrows an amount of money, called the principal, from the _____, and is obligated to pay back or repay an equal amount of money to the _____ at a later time.

   a. Credit rating
   b. Debt
   c. Lender
   d. Loan to value

10. In financial accounting, a _____ or Statement of cash flows is a financial statement that shows a company's flow of cash. The money coming into the business is called cash inflow, and money going out from the business is called cash outflow. The statement shows how changes in balance sheet and income accounts affect cash and cash equivalents, and breaks the analysis down to operating, investing, and financing activities.
   a. BMC Software, Inc.
   b. 3M Company
   c. BNSF Railway
   d. Cash flow statement

4 *Chapter 1. Accounting Information: Users and Uses*

11. _____ is the balance of the amounts of cash being received and paid by a business during a defined period of time, sometimes tied to a specific project. Measurement of _____ can be used

- to evaluate the state or performance of a business or project.
- to determine problems with liquidity. Being profitable does not necessarily mean being liquid. A company can fail because of a shortage of cash, even while profitable.
- to project rate of returns. The time of _____s into and out of projects are used as inputs to financial models such as internal rate of return, and net present value.
- to examine income or growth of a business when it is believed that accrual accounting concepts do not represent economic realities. Alternately, _____ can be used to 'validate' the net income generated by accrual accounting.

_____ as a generic term may be used differently depending on context, and certain _____ definitions may be adapted by analysts and users for their own uses. Common terms include operating _____ and free _____.

a. Commercial paper
b. Cash flow
c. Flow-through entity
d. Controlling interest

12. A _____, also client, buyer or purchaser is the buyer or user of the paid products of an individual or organization, mostly called the supplier or seller. This is typically through purchasing or renting goods or services.
a. Customer
b. BNSF Railway
c. 3M Company
d. BMC Software, Inc.

13. Employment is a contract between two parties, one being the employer and the other being the _____. An _____ may be defined as: 'A person in the service of another under any contract of hire, express or implied, oral or written, where the employer has the power or right to control and direct the _____ in the material details of how the work is to be performed.' Black's Law Dictionary page 471 (5th ed. 1979.)
a. ABC Television Network
b. AIG
c. AMEX
d. Employee

14. A _____ is a permanent or semi-permanent organization in the machinery of government that is responsible for the oversight and administration of specific functions, such as an intelligence agency. There is a notable variety of types of agency. Although usage differs, a _____ is normally distinct both from a Department or Ministry, and other types of public body established by government.

Chapter 1. Accounting Information: Users and Uses

a. BMC Software, Inc.
b. 3M Company
c. BNSF Railway
d. Government agency

15. The United States _____ is an independent, non-partisan, quasi-judicial, federal agency of the United States that provides trade expertise to both the legislative and executive branches. Further, the agency determines the impact of imports on U.S. industries and directs actions against certain unfair trade practices, such as dumping, patent, trademark, and copyright infringement.

The USInternational Trade Commission was established by the U.S. Congress in 1916 as the U.S. Tariff Commission (the Trade Act of 1974 changed its name to the U.S. _____), the agency has broad investigative powers on matters of trade.

a. ABC Television Network
b. AIG
c. AMEX
d. International Trade Commission

16. A _____ is a fungible, negotiable instrument representing financial value. they are broadly categorized into debt securities (such as banknotes, bonds and debentures), and equity securities; e.g., common stocks. The company or other entity issuing the _____ is called the issuer.

a. 3M Company
b. Security
c. BMC Software, Inc.
d. Tracking stock

17. The U.S. _____ is an independent agency of the United States government which holds primary responsibility for enforcing the federal securities laws and regulating the securities industry, the nation's stock and options exchanges, and other electronic securities markets. The SEC was created by section 4 of the Securities Exchange Act of 1934 (now codified as 15 U.S.C. ÂÂ§ 78d and commonly referred to as the 1934 Act.)

a. BMC Software, Inc.
b. 3M Company
c. Securities and Exchange Commission
d. BNSF Railway

Chapter 1. Accounting Information: Users and Uses

18. The _____ is a private, not-for-profit organization whose primary purpose is to develop generally accepted accounting principles (GAAP) within the United States in the public's interest. The Securities and Exchange Commission (SEC) designated the _____ as the organization responsible for setting accounting standards for public companies in the U.S. It was created in 1973, replacing the Accounting Principles Board and the Committee on Accounting Procedure of the American Institute of Certified Public Accountants. The _____'s mission is 'to establish and improve standards of financial accounting and reporting for the guidance and education of the public, including issuers, auditors, and users of financial information.'

The _____ is not a governmental body.

   a. Governmental Accounting Standards Board
   b. Financial Accounting Standards Board
   c. Fannie Mae
   d. Public company

19. _____ is the term used to refer to the standard framework of guidelines for financial accounting used in any given jurisdiction. _____ includes the standards, conventions, and rules accountants follow in recording and summarizing transactions, and in the preparation of financial statements.

Financial accounting information must be assembled and reported objectively.

   a. General ledger
   b. Long-term liabilities
   c. Current asset
   d. Generally accepted accounting principles

20. An _____ is a practitioner of accountancy, which is the measurement, disclosure or provision of assurance about financial information that helps managers, investors, tax authorities and other decision makers make resource allocation decisions.

The word '_____' is derived from the French 'Compter' which took its origin from the Latin 'Computare'. The word was formerly written in English as 'Accomptant', but in process of time the word, which was always pronounced by dropping the 'p', became gradually changed both in pronunciation and in orthography to its present form.

   a. ABC Television Network
   b. AMEX
   c. AIG
   d. Accountant

Chapter 1. Accounting Information: Users and Uses

21. The _____ is the national, professional association of CPAs in the United States, with more than 330,000 members, including CPAs in business and industry, public practice, government, and education; student affiliates; and international associates. It sets ethical standards for the profession and U.S. auditing standards for audits of private companies; federal, state and local governments; and non-profit organizations.

Approximately 40% of its members are engaged in the practice of public accounting, in areas such as auditing, accounting, taxation, general business consulting, business valuation, personal financial planning and business technology.

   a. Other postemployment benefits
   b. ABC Television Network
   c. AIG
   d. American Institute of Certified Public Accountants

22. _____ is the statutory title of qualified accountants in the United States who have passed the Uniform _____ Examination and have met additional state education and experience requirements for certification as a _____. Individuals who have passed the Exam but have not either accomplished the required on-the-job experience or have previously met it but in the meantime have lapsed their continuing professional education are, in many states, permitted the designation '_____ Inactive' or an equivalent phrase. In most U.S. states, only _____s who are licensed are able to provide to the public attestation (including auditing) opinions on financial statements.
   a. Certified Public Accountant
   b. Chartered Accountant
   c. Chartered Certified Accountant
   d. Certified General Accountant

23. An _____ is a term used in behavioral economics to describe those types of behaviors that impose costs on a person in the long-run that are not taken into account when making decisions in the present. Classical Economics discourages government from creating legislation that targets internalities, because it is assumed that the consumer takes these personal costs into account when paying for the good that causes the _____. For example, cigarettes should be taxed because of the negative consumption externalities that they impose, such as second-hand smoke, not because the smoker harms him or herself by smoking.
   a. Operating budget
   b. Authorised capital
   c. Inventory turnover ratio
   d. Internality

24. The _____ is the United States federal government agency that collects taxes and enforces the internal revenue laws. It is an agency within the U.S. Dept of the treasury responsible for interpretation and application of Federal tax law. The official U.S. Treasury regulations provide (in part):

The _____ is a bureau of the Department of the Treasury under the immediate direction of the Commissioner of Internal Revenue.

   a. Internal Revenue Service
   b. Use tax
   c. Indirect tax
   d. Income tax

25. The term _____ usually refers to a company that is permitted to offer its registered securities (stock, bonds, etc.) for sale to the general public, typically through a stock exchange, or occasionally a company whose stock is traded over the counter (OTC) via market makers who use non-exchange quotation services.

The term '_____' may also refer to a company owned by the government.

   a. MicroStrategy
   b. Governmental Accounting Standards Board
   c. Professional association
   d. Public Company

26. The _____ (sometimes called 'Peekaboo') is a private-sector, non-profit corporation created by the Sarbanes-Oxley Act, a 2002 United States federal law, to oversee the auditors of public companies. Its stated purpose is to 'protect the interests of investors and further the public interest in the preparation of informative, fair, and independent audit reports'. Although a private entity, the _____ has many government-like regulatory functions, making it in some ways similar to the private Self Regulatory Organizations (SROs) that regulate stock markets and other aspects of the financial markets in the United States.
   a. Public Company Accounting Oversight Board
   b. 3M Company
   c. Pension Benefit Guaranty Corporation
   d. Financial Crimes Enforcement Network

Chapter 1. Accounting Information: Users and Uses

27. The _____ of 2002 (Pub.L. 107-204, 116 Stat. 745, enacted July 30, 2002), also known as the Public Company Accounting Reform and Investor Protection Act of 2002, is a United States federal law enacted on July 30, 2002 in response to a number of major corporate and accounting scandals including those affecting Enron, Tyco International, Adelphia, Peregrine Systems and WorldCom. The legislation establishes new or enhanced standards for all U.S. public company boards, management, and public accounting firms. It does not apply to privately held companies.

   a. Fair Labor Standards Act
   b. Sarbanes-Oxley Act
   c. FCPA
   d. Lease

28. The _____ founded on April 1, 2001 is the successor of the International Accounting Standards Committee (IASC) founded in June 1973 in London. It is responsible for developing the International Financial Reporting Standards (new name for the International Accounting Standards issued after 2001), and promoting the use and application of these standards.

   The _____ is an independent, privately-funded accounting standard-setter based in London, UK.

   a. Information Systems Audit and Control Association
   b. Emerging technologies
   c. Institute of Management Accountants
   d. International Accounting Standards Board

29. _____ are standards and interpretations adopted by the International Accounting Standards Board (IASB.)

   Many of the standards forming part of _____ are known by the older name of International Accounting Standards (IAS.) IAS were issued between 1973 and 2001 by the board of the International Accounting Standards Committee (IASC.)

   a. Out-of-pocket
   b. International Financial Reporting Standards
   c. ABC Television Network
   d. AIG

30. The _____, a unit of the United States Department of Labor, is the principal fact-finding agency for the U.S. government in the broad field of labor economics and statistics. The _____ is an independent national statistical agency that collects, processes, analyzes, and disseminates essential statistical data to the American public, the U.S. Congress, other Federal agencies, State and local governments, business, and labor representatives.

a. 3M Company
b. BNSF Railway
c. Bureau of Labor Statistics
d. BMC Software, Inc.

31. _____ is a mathematical science pertaining to the collection, analysis, interpretation or explanation, and presentation of data. It also provides tools for prediction and forecasting based on data. It is applicable to a wide variety of academic disciplines, from the natural and social sciences to the humanities, government and business.

a. Statistics
b. Probability distribution
c. Variance
d. Time series

Chapter 2. Financial Statements: An Overview

1. In financial accounting, a _____ or statement of financial position is a summary of a person's or organization's balances. Assets, liabilities and ownership equity are listed as of a specific date, such as the end of its financial year. A _____ is often described as a snapshot of a company's financial condition.
    a. Financial statements
    b. 3M Company
    c. Balance sheet
    d. Statement of retained earnings

2. _____ is a company's financial statement that indicates how the revenue is transformed into the net income The purpose of the _____ is to show managers and investors whether the company made or lost money during the period being reported.

The important thing to remember about an _____ is that it represents a period of time.

    a. AIG
    b. AMEX
    c. ABC Television Network
    d. Income statement

3. In financial accounting, a _____ or Statement of cash flows is a financial statement that shows a company's flow of cash. The money coming into the business is called cash inflow, and money going out from the business is called cash outflow. The statement shows how changes in balance sheet and income accounts affect cash and cash equivalents, and breaks the analysis down to operating, investing, and financing activities.
    a. 3M Company
    b. BNSF Railway
    c. Cash flow statement
    d. BMC Software, Inc.

4. _____ is the balance of the amounts of cash being received and paid by a business during a defined period of time, sometimes tied to a specific project. Measurement of _____ can be used

   - to evaluate the state or performance of a business or project.
   - to determine problems with liquidity. Being profitable does not necessarily mean being liquid. A company can fail because of a shortage of cash, even while profitable.
   - to project rate of returns. The time of _____s into and out of projects are used as inputs to financial models such as internal rate of return, and net present value.
   - to examine income or growth of a business when it is believed that accrual accounting concepts do not represent economic realities. Alternately, _____ can be used to 'validate' the net income generated by accrual accounting.

Chapter 2. Financial Statements: An Overview

_____ as a generic term may be used differently depending on context, and certain _____ definitions may be adapted by analysts and users for their own uses. Common terms include operating _____ and free _____.

  a. Controlling interest
  b. Cash flow
  c. Commercial paper
  d. Flow-through entity

5. _____ is a specific term used in companies' financial reporting from the company-whole point of view. Because that use excludes the effects of changing ownership interest, an economic measure of _____ is necessary for financial analysis from the shareholders' point of view

_____ is defined by the Financial Accounting Standards Board, or FASB, as 'the change in equity [net assets] of a business enterprise during a period from transactions and other events and circumstances from nonowner sources. It includes all changes in equity during a period except those resulting from investments by owners and distributions to owners.'

_____ is the sum of net income and other items that must bypass the income statement because they have not been realized, including items like an unrealized holding gain or loss from available for sale securities and foreign currency translation gains or losses.

  a. Comprehensive income
  b. BNSF Railway
  c. 3M Company
  d. BMC Software, Inc.

6. _____ are formal records of a business' financial activities.

In British English, including United Kingdom company law, _____ are often referred to as accounts, although the term _____ is also used, particularly by accountants.

_____ provide an overview of a business' financial condition in both short and long term.

  a. Notes to the financial statements
  b. Statement of retained earnings
  c. 3M Company
  d. Financial statements

7. In business and accounting, _____ are everything of value that is owned by a person or company. It is a claim on the property your income of a borrower. The balance sheet of a firm records the monetary value of the _____ owned by the firm.
   a. Earnings before interest, taxes, depreciation and amortization
   b. Accounts receivable
   c. Accrual basis accounting
   d. Assets

8. In financial accounting, a _____ is defined as an obligation of an entity arising from past transactions or events, the settlement of which may result in the transfer or use of assets, provision of services or other yielding of economic benefits in the future.
   a. Corporate governance
   b. Liability
   c. Vested
   d. False Claims Act

9. _____ is a process by which a firm can obtain the use of a certain fixed assets for which it must pay a series of contractual, periodic, tax deductable payments. The lessee is the receiver of the services or the assets under the lease contract and the lessor is the owner of the assets. The relationship between the tenant and the landlord is called a tenancy, and can be for a fixed or an indefinite period of time (called the term of the lease.)
   a. Federal Sentencing Guidelines
   b. Leasing
   c. Property
   d. Resource Conservation and Recovery Act

10. _____ are sometimes the same as net worth, or shareholders' equity - assets minus liabilities. The term _____ is commonly used with charities or not for profit entities. Although these entities don't make money, it is important to maintain reasonable reserves to help future growth.
    a. Net interest spread
    b. Debtor days
    c. Sortino ratio
    d. Net assets

11. The basic _____ is the foundation for the double-entry bookkeeping system. It shows how assets were financed: either by borrowing money from someone (liability) or by paying your own money (shareholders' equity.)

   Assets = Liabilities + (Shareholders or Owners equity)

For example: A student buys a computer for $945.

a. ABC Television Network
b. AIG
c. AMEX
d. Accounting equation

12. In economics, _____ or _____ goods or real _____ refers to factors of production used to create goods or services that are not themselves significantly consumed (though they may depreciate) in the production process. _____ goods may be acquired with money or financial _____. In finance and accounting, _____ generally refers to financial wealth, especially that used to start or maintain a business.

a. Vyborg Appeal
b. Disclosure
c. Capital
d. Screening

13. _____ is the planning process used to determine whether a firm's long term investments such as new machinery, replacement machinery, new plants, new products, and research development projects are worth pursuing. It is budget for major capital, or investment, expenditures.

Many formal methods are used in _____, including the techniques such as

- Net present value
- Profitability index
- Internal rate of return
- Modified Internal Rate of Return
- Equivalent annuity

These methods use the incremental cash flows from each potential investment, or project. Techniques based on accounting earnings and accounting rules are sometimes used - though economists consider this to be improper - such as the accounting rate of return, and 'return on investment.' Simplified and hybrid methods are used as well, such as payback period and discounted payback period.

a. Cash flow
b. Gross profit
c. Capital budgeting
d. Preferred stock

14. _____ are payments made by a corporation to its shareholder members. It is the portion of corporate profits paid out to stockholders. When a corporation earns a profit or surplus, that money can be put to two uses: it can either be re-invested in the business (called retained earnings), or it can be paid to the shareholders as a dividend.

   a. Dividend yield
   b. Dividend stripping
   c. Dividend payout ratio
   d. Dividends

15. _____ is a system of financial accounting where each transaction is recorded in at least two accounts: at least one account is debited and at least one account is credited, so that the total debits of the transaction equal to the total credits. For example, if Company A sells an item to Company B, and Company B pays by cheque, then the bookkeeper of Company A credits the account 'Sales' and debits the account 'Bank'. Conversely, the bookkeeper of Company B debits the account 'Purchases' and credits the account 'Bank'.

   a. Debit and credit
   b. Double-entry bookkeeping
   c. Cookie jar accounting
   d. Bookkeeping

16. A mutual shareholder or _____ is an individual or company (including a corporation) that legally owns one or more shares of stock in a joint stock company. A company's shareholders collectively own that company. Thus, the typical goal of such companies is to enhance shareholder value.

   a. Growth investing
   b. 3M Company
   c. Stock split
   d. Stockholder

17. A _____ is the transfer of wealth from one party (such as a person or company) to another. A _____ is usually made in exchange for the provision of goods, services or both, or to fulfill a legal obligation.

   The simplest and oldest form of _____ is barter, the exchange of one good or service for another.

   a. Payment
   b. BMC Software, Inc.
   c. Payee
   d. 3M Company

18. In accounting, a _____ is an asset on the balance sheet which is expected to be sold or otherwise used up in the near future, usually within one year, or one business cycle - whichever is longer. Typical _____s include cash, cash equivalents, accounts receivable, inventory, the portion of prepaid accounts which will be used within a year, and short-term investments.

On the balance sheet, assets will typically be classified into _____s and long-term assets.

a. Deferred
b. General ledger
c. Pro forma
d. Current asset

19. In accounting, _____ are considered liabilities of the business that are to be settled in cash within the fiscal year or the operating cycle, whichever period is longer.

For example accounts payable for goods, services or supplies that were purchased for use in the operation of the business and payable within a normal period of time would be _____.

Bonds, mortgages and loans that are payable over a term exceeding one year would be fixed liabilities.

a. Payroll
b. Current liabilities
c. Closing entries
d. Treasury stock

20. _____ is a business, economics or investment term that refers to an asset's ability to be easily converted through an act of buying or selling without causing a significant movement in the price and with minimum loss of value. Money, or cash on hand, is the most liquid asset. An act of exchange of a less liquid asset with a more liquid asset is called liquidation.

a. Transfer agent
b. Spot rate
c. Financial instruments
d. Market liquidity

21. In economic models, the _____ time frame assumes no fixed factors of production. Firms can enter or leave the marketplace, and the cost (and availability) of land, labor, raw materials, and capital goods can be assumed to vary. In contrast, in the short-run time frame, certain factors are assumed to be fixed, because there is not sufficient time for them to change.

a. Short-run
b. BMC Software, Inc.
c. 3M Company
d. Long-run

22. _____ are liabilities with a future benefit over one year, such as notes payable that mature greater than one year.

In accounting, the _____ are shown on the right wing of the balance-sheet representing the sources of funds, which are generally bounded in form of capital assets.

Examples of _____ are debentures, mortgage loans and other bank loans (note: not all bank loans are long term as not all are paid over a period greater than a year, the example is bridging loan.)

a. Cash basis accounting
b. Book value
c. Gross sales
d. Long-term liabilities

23. A _____ is any one of a variety of different systems, institutions, procedures, social relations and infrastructures whereby persons trade, and goods and services are exchanged, forming part of the economy. It is an arrangement that allows buyers and sellers to exchange things. _____s vary in size, range, geographic scale, location, types and variety of human communities, as well as the types of goods and services traded.
a. Market Failure
b. Perfect competition
c. Market
d. Recession

24. _____ is the price at which an asset would trade in a competitive Walrasian auction setting. _____ is often used interchangeably with open _____, fair value or fair _____, although these terms have distinct definitions in different standards, and may differ in some circumstances.

International Valuation Standards defines _____ as 'the estimated amount for which a property should exchange on the date of valuation between a willing buyer and a willing seller in an arme;s-length transaction after proper marketing wherein the parties had each acted knowledgeably, prudently, and without compulsion.'

_____ is a concept distinct from market price, which is e;the price at which one can transacte;, while _____ is e;the true underlying valuee; according to theoretical standards.

a. Sinking fund
b. Debtor
c. Segregated portfolio company
d. Market value

25. In finance, a _____ is a debt security, in which the authorized issuer owes the holders a debt and, depending on the terms of the _____, is obliged to pay interest (the coupon) and/or to repay the principal at a later date, termed maturity. It is a formal contract to repay borrowed money with interest at fixed intervals.

Thus a _____ is like a loan: the issuer is the borrower, the _____ holder is the lender, and the coupon is the interest.

a. Coupon rate
b. Zero-coupon bond
c. Bond
d. Revenue bonds

26. In accounting, _____ or carrying value is the value of an asset according to its balance sheet account balance. For assets, the value is based on the original cost of the asset less any depreciation, amortization or impairment costs made against the asset. Traditionally, a company's _____ is its total assets minus intangible assets and liabilities.

a. Matching principle
b. Generally accepted accounting principles
c. Depreciation
d. Book value

27. In financial accounting and finance, _____ is the portion of receivables that can no longer be collected, typically from accounts receivable or loans. _____ in accounting is considered an expense.

There are two methods to account for _____:

1. Direct write off method (Non - GAAP)

A receivable which is not considered collectible is charged directly to the income statement.

1. Allowance method (GAAP)

An estimate is made at the end of each fiscal year of the amount of _____. This is then accumulated in a provision which is then used to reduce specific receivable accounts as and when necessary.

a. 3M Company
b. Bad debt
c. Total Expense Ratio
d. Tax expense

28. _____ is that which is owed; usually referencing assets owed, but the term can also cover moral obligations and other interactions not requiring money. In the case of assets, _____ is a means of using future purchasing power in the present before a summation has been earned. Some companies and corporations use _____ as a part of their overall corporate finance strategy.
    a. Lender
    b. Debenture
    c. Debt
    d. Loan

29. _____ is equal to the income that a firm has after subtracting costs and expenses from the total revenue. _____ can be distributed among holders of common stock as a dividend or held by the firm as retained earnings.

The items deducted will typically include tax expense, financing expense (interest expense), and minority interest. Likewise, preferred stock dividends will be subtracted too, though they are not an expense.

   a. Generally accepted accounting principles
   b. Matching principle
   c. Net income
   d. Long-term liabilities

30. _____ of something is, in finance, the adding together of interest or different investments over a period of time such as atoms (1 - the act or process of accruing; 2 - the amount that accrues.) It holds specific meanings in accounting and payroll.

_____, in accounting, describes the accounting method known as _____ basis, whereby revenues and expenses are recognized when they are accrued, i.e. accumulated (earned or incurred), regardless when the actual cash is received or paid out.

   a. Accounts receivable
   b. Earnings before interest, taxes, depreciation and amortization
   c. Assets
   d. Accrual

31. _____ are the earnings returned on the initial investment amount.

In the US, the Financial Accounting Standards Board (FASB) requires companies' income statements to report _____ for each of the major categories of the income statement: continuing operations, discontinued operations, extraordinary items, and net income.

The _____ formula does not include preferred dividends for categories outside of continued operations and net income.

a. Invested capital
b. Earnings yield
c. Average accounting return
d. Earnings per share

32. In accounting, _____ or sales profit is the difference between revenue and the cost of making a product or providing a service, before deducting overhead, payroll, taxation, and interest payments. Note that this is different from operating profit (earnings before interest and taxes.)

Net sales are calculated:

Net sales = Sales - Sales returns and allowances.

a. Commercial paper
b. Participating preferred stock
c. Capital structure
d. Gross profit

33. _____, Gross profit margin or Gross Profit Rate can be defined as the amount of contribution to the business enterprise, after paying for direct-fixed and direct-variable unit costs, required to cover overheads (fixed commitments) and provide a buffer for unknown items. It expresses the relationship between gross profit and sales revenue.

It can be expressed in absolute terms:

Gross Profit = Revenue − Cost of Goods Sold

or as the ratio of gross profit to sales revenue, usually in the form of a percentage:

_____ Percentage = (Revenue-Cost of Goods Sold)/Revenue

Cost of goods sold includes variable costs and fixed costs directly linked to the product, such as material and labor.

Chapter 2. Financial Statements: An Overview

a. BMC Software, Inc.
b. Gross margin
c. 3M Company
d. BNSF Railway

34. The _____ is one of the basic financial statements as per Generally Accepted Accounting Principles, and it explains the changes in a company's retained earnings over the reporting period. It breaks down changes affecting the account, such as profits or losses from operations, dividends paid, and any other items charged or credited to retained earnings. A retained earnings statement is required by Generally Accepted Accounting Principles whenever comparative balance sheets and income statements are presented.
   a. 3M Company
   b. Statement of retained earnings
   c. Financial statements
   d. Notes to the financial statements

35. In vector calculus, _____ is a vector differential operator represented by the nabla symbol: ∇.

_____ is a mathematical tool serving primarily as a convention for mathematical notation; it makes many equations easier to comprehend, write, and remember. Depending on the way _____ is applied, it can describe the gradient (slope), divergence (degree to which something converges or diverges) or curl (rotational motion at points in a fluid.)

   a. 3M Company
   b. BNSF Railway
   c. BMC Software, Inc.
   d. Del

36. _____ are additional notes and information added to the end of the financial statements to supplement the reader with more information. Notes to Financial Statements help explain the computation of specific items in the financial statements as well as provide a more comprehensive assessment of a company's financial condition. Notes to Financial Statements can include information on debt, going concern, accounts, contingent liabilities, or contextual information explaining the financial numbers (e.g. to indicate a lawsuit.)
   a. Statement of retained earnings
   b. Financial statements
   c. 3M Company
   d. Notes to the financial statements

37. _____ means the giving out of information, either voluntarily or to be in compliance with legal regulations or workplace rules.

- In Computer security, full _____ means disclosing full information about vulnerabilities.
- In computing, _____ widget
- Journalism, full _____ refers to disclosing the interests of the writer which may bear on the subject being written about, for example, if the writer has worked with an interview subject in the past.

- In law:
    - The law of England and Wales, _____ refers to a process that may form part of legal proceedings, whereby parties inform to other parties the existence of any relevant documents that are, or have been, in their control. This compares with the process known as discovery in the course of legal proceedings in the United States.
    - In U.S. civil procedure (litigation rules for civil cases), _____ is a stage prior to trial. In civil cases, each party must disclose to the opposing party the following: names of witnesses which it may use to support its side, copies of documents (or mere description of these documents) in its control which it may use to support its side, computation of damages claimed, and certain insurance information. _____ is related to, but technically prior to, the discovery stage.
    - In Company law (known as 'corporate law' in the United States), _____ refers to giving out information about public or limited companies or their officers, which might be kept secret if the company was a private company or a partnership.

- In real property transactions, _____ refers to providing to a buyer information known to the seller or broker/agent concerning the condition or other aspects of real property that would affect the property's value or desirability. These rules regarding what information must be disclosed, and whether the information must be disclosed even if a buyer does not ask, vary from one jurisdiction to the next.

a. Trailing
b. Controlled Foreign Corporations
c. Disclosure
d. Tax harmonisation

38. An _____ is a practitioner of accountancy, which is the measurement, disclosure or provision of assurance about financial information that helps managers, investors, tax authorities and other decision makers make resource allocation decisions.

The word '_____' is derived from the French 'Compter' which took its origin from the Latin 'Computare'. The word was formerly written in English as 'Accomptant', but in process of time the word, which was always pronounced by dropping the 'p', became gradually changed both in pronunciation and in orthography to its present form.

a. AIG
b. AMEX
c. ABC Television Network
d. Accountant

39. The general definition of an _____ is an evaluation of a person, organization, system, process, project or product. _____s are performed to ascertain the validity and reliability of information; also to provide an assessment of a system's internal control. The goal of an _____ is to express an opinion on the person/organization/system (etc) in question, under evaluation based on work done on a test basis.
   a. Audit
   b. Assurance service
   c. Institute of Chartered Accountants of India
   d. Audit regime

40. _____ is the statutory title of qualified accountants in the United States who have passed the Uniform _____ Examination and have met additional state education and experience requirements for certification as a _____. Individuals who have passed the Exam but have not either accomplished the required on-the-job experience or have previously met it but in the meantime have lapsed their continuing professional education are, in many states, permitted the designation '_____ Inactive' or an equivalent phrase. In most U.S. states, only _____s who are licensed are able to provide to the public attestation (including auditing) opinions on financial statements.
   a. Chartered Certified Accountant
   b. Certified public accountant
   c. Certified General Accountant
   d. Chartered Accountant

41. _____ is an acronym for First In, First Out, an abstraction in ways of organizing and manipulation of data relative to time and prioritization. This expression describes the principle of a queue processing technique or servicing conflicting demands by ordering process by first-come, first-served (FCFS) behaviour: what comes in first is handled first, what comes in next waits until the first is finished, etc.

Thus it is analogous to the behaviour of persons queueing (or 'standing in line', in common American parlance), where the persons leave the queue in the order they arrive, or waiting one's turn at a traffic control signal.

   a. Kanban
   b. Risk management
   c. Trademark
   d. FIFO

42. In economics, business, retail, and accounting, a _____ is the value of money that has been used up to produce something, and hence is not available for use anymore. In economics, a _____ is an alternative that is given up as a result of a decision. In business, the _____ may be one of acquisition, in which case the amount of money expended to acquire it is counted as _____.
   a. Cost of quality
   b. Cost allocation
   c. Prime cost
   d. Cost

43. _____ methods are means of managing inventory and financial matters involving the money a company ties up within inventory of produced goods, raw materials, parts, components, or feed stocks. FIFO stands for first-in, first-out, meaning that the oldest inventory items are recorded as sold first. LIFO stands for last-in, first-out, meaning that the most recently purchased items are recorded as sold first.
   a. 3M Company
   b. Finished good
   c. Reorder point
   d. FIFO and LIFO accounting

44. _____ was a maxim coined by Josiah Warren, indicating a (prescriptive) version of the labor theory of value. Warren maintained that the just compensation for labor (or for its product) could only be an equivalent amount of labor (or a product embodying an equivalent amount.) Thus, profit, rent, and interest were considered unjust economic arrangements.
   a. 3M Company
   b. BMC Software, Inc.
   c. Politicized issue
   d. Cost the limit of price

45. A _____ is a business that functions without the intention or threat of liquidation for the foreseeable future, usually regarded as at least within 12 months.

In accounting, '_____' refers to a company's ability to continue functioning as a business entity. It is the responsibility of the directors to assess whether the _____ assumption is appropriate when preparing the financial statements.

   a. Payment
   b. BMC Software, Inc.
   c. 3M Company
   d. Going concern

46. In accounting, _____ is the original monetary value of an economic item. In some circumstances, assets and liabilities may be shown at their _____, as if there had been no change in value since the date of acquisition. The balance sheet value of the item may therefore differ from the 'true' value.
   a. Cost of goods sold
   b. Bottom line
   c. Matching principle
   d. Historical cost

Chapter 3. The Mechanics of Accounting

1. An _____ invented by esteemed professor Karen Osterheld is the system of records a business keeps to maintain its accounting system. This includes the purchase, sales, and other financial processes of the business. The purpose of an _____ is to accumulate data and provide decision makers (investors, creditors, and managers) with information to make decision While this was previously a paper-based process, most modern businesses now use accounting software such as UBS, MYOB etc.

    a. AIG
    b. ABC Television Network
    c. AMEX
    d. Accounting information system

2. The basic _____ is the foundation for the double-entry bookkeeping system. It shows how assets were financed: either by borrowing money from someone (liability) or by paying your own money (shareholders' equity.)

    Assets = Liabilities + (Shareholders or Owners equity)

    For example: A student buys a computer for $945.

    a. Accounting equation
    b. AIG
    c. ABC Television Network
    d. AMEX

3. In economics, the _____, (or _____) measures the payments that flow between any individual country and all other countries. It is used to summarize all international economic transactions for that country during a specific time period, usually a year. The _____ is determined by the country's exports and imports of goods, services, and financial capital, as well as financial transfers.

    a. Stock split
    b. Yield to maturity
    c. Moving average
    d. Balance of payments

4. An _____ is a practitioner of accountancy, which is the measurement, disclosure or provision of assurance about financial information that helps managers, investors, tax authorities and other decision makers make resource allocation decisions.

The word '_____' is derived from the French 'Compter' which took its origin from the Latin 'Computare'. The word was formerly written in English as 'Accomptant', but in process of time the word, which was always pronounced by dropping the 'p', became gradually changed both in pronunciation and in orthography to its present form.

Chapter 3. The Mechanics of Accounting 27

   a. Accountant
   b. AMEX
   c. AIG
   d. ABC Television Network

5. _____ and credit are formal bookkeeping and accounting terms. They are the most fundamental concepts in accounting, representing the two records that one party in a transaction makes on its records, transferring a money balance from one account to another, one representing a reduction of liability or increase in asset, and the other representing a balancing increase in liability or reduction of asset.

Introduction

_____s and credits are a system of notation used in accounting to keep track of money movements (transactions) into and out of an account.

   a. Bookkeeping
   b. Cookie jar accounting
   c. Debit
   d. Debit and credit

6. The term _____, derived from the distinctive T shape, is frequently used when discussing or analyzing accounting or business transactions. _____s are used to represent general ledger accounts.

Typically one or more Ts are drawn on a white board or blank piece of paper. A general ledger account name or number is then written above each T. Debit entries are recorded on the left side of the 'T' and credit entries are recorded on the right side of the 'T'.

   a. BMC Software, Inc.
   b. 3M Company
   c. BNSF Railway
   d. T account

7. A _____, also client, buyer or purchaser is the buyer or user of the paid products of an individual or organization, mostly called the supplier or seller. This is typically through purchasing or renting goods or services.
   a. Customer
   b. 3M Company
   c. BMC Software, Inc.
   d. BNSF Railway

Chapter 3. The Mechanics of Accounting

8. _____ are payments made by a corporation to its shareholder members. It is the portion of corporate profits paid out to stockholders. When a corporation earns a profit or surplus, that money can be put to two uses: it can either be re-invested in the business (called retained earnings), or it can be paid to the shareholders as a dividend.
   a. Dividends
   b. Dividend stripping
   c. Dividend yield
   d. Dividend payout ratio

9. In financial accounting and finance, _____ is the portion of receivables that can no longer be collected, typically from accounts receivable or loans. _____ in accounting is considered an expense.

There are two methods to account for _____:

   1. Direct write off method (Non - GAAP)

A receivable which is not considered collectible is charged directly to the income statement.

   1. Allowance method (GAAP)

An estimate is made at the end of each fiscal year of the amount of _____. This is then accumulated in a provision which is then used to reduce specific receivable accounts as and when necessary.

   a. Bad debt
   b. Tax expense
   c. Total Expense Ratio
   d. 3M Company

10. _____ is that which is owed; usually referencing assets owed, but the term can also cover moral obligations and other interactions not requiring money. In the case of assets, _____ is a means of using future purchasing power in the present before a summation has been earned. Some companies and corporations use _____ as a part of their overall corporate finance strategy.
    a. Debenture
    b. Loan
    c. Lender
    d. Debt

11. In accounting, _____ has a very specific meaning. It is an outflow of cash or other valuable assets from a person or company to another person or company. This outflow of cash is generally one side of a trade for products or services that have equal or better current or future value to the buyer than to the seller.

Chapter 3. The Mechanics of Accounting 29

a. Expense
b. ABC Television Network
c. AMEX
d. AIG

12. A _____ is the transfer of wealth from one party (such as a person or company) to another. A _____ is usually made in exchange for the provision of goods, services or both, or to fulfill a legal obligation.

The simplest and oldest form of _____ is barter, the exchange of one good or service for another.

a. Payee
b. 3M Company
c. BMC Software, Inc.
d. Payment

13. A _____ has several related meanings:

- a daily record of events or business; a private _____ is usually referred to as a diary.
- a newspaper or other periodical, in the literal sense of one published each day;
- many publications issued at stated intervals, such as magazines, or scholarly academic _____s, or the record of the transactions of a society, are often called _____s. Although _____ is sometimes used, erroneously, as a synonym for 'magazine,' in academic use, a _____ refers to a serious, scholarly publication, most often peer-reviewed. A non-scholarly magazine written for an educated audience about an industry or an area of professional activity is usually called a professional magazine.

The word 'journalist' for one whose business is writing for the public press has been in use since the end of the 17th century.

Open access _____s are scholarly _____s that are available to the reader without financial or other barrier other than access to the internet itself. Some are subsidized, and some require payment on behalf of the author. Subsidized _____s are financed by an academic institution or a government information center.

a. BMC Software, Inc.
b. BNSF Railway
c. Journal
d. 3M Company

14. The _____ is where double entry bookkeeping entries are recorded by debiting one account and crediting another account with the same amount. The amount debited and the amount credited should always be equal, thereby ensuring the accounting equation is maintained.

Depending on the business's accounting information system, specialized journals may be used in conjunction with the _____ for record-keeping.

   a. Sales journal
   b. General ledger
   c. Journal entry
   d. General journal

15. _____ is the state or fact of exclusive rights and control over property, which may be an object, land/real estate or intellectual property. An _____ right is also referred to as title.

_____ is the key building block in the development of the capitalist socio-economic system.

   a. Ownership
   b. Encumbrance
   c. ABC Television Network
   d. Administrative proceeding

16. In business and accounting, _____ are everything of value that is owned by a person or company. It is a claim on the property your income of a borrower. The balance sheet of a firm records the monetary value of the _____ owned by the firm.
   a. Accounts receivable
   b. Earnings before interest, taxes, depreciation and amortization
   c. Accrual basis accounting
   d. Assets

17. _____ is a process by which a firm can obtain the use of a certain fixed assets for which it must pay a series of contractual, periodic, tax deductable payments. The lessee is the receiver of the services or the assets under the lease contract and the lessor is the owner of the assets. The relationship between the tenant and the landlord is called a tenancy, and can be for a fixed or an indefinite period of time (called the term of the lease.)
   a. Property
   b. Leasing
   c. Resource Conservation and Recovery Act
   d. Federal Sentencing Guidelines

Chapter 3. The Mechanics of Accounting 31

18. A _____, in accounting, is a logging of transcriptions into items accounting journal. The _____ can consist of several items, each of which is either a debit or a credit. The total of the debits must equal the total of the credits, or the _____ is said to be 'unbalanced.' Journal entries can record unique items or recurring items such as depreciation or bond amortization.

   a. Sales journal
   b. General ledger
   c. General journal
   d. Journal entry

19. _____ is a list of the accounts including a unique number of each allowing to locate it in each ledger. The list is typically arranged in the order of the customary appearance of accounts in the financial statements. A _____ can track a specific financial information.

   a. Journal entry
   b. General journal
   c. General ledger
   d. Chart of accounts

20. In accounting, the _____ is a worksheet listing the balance at a certain date, of each ledger account in two columns, namely debit and credit. Under the double-entry system, in any transaction the total of any debits must equal the total of any credits, so in a _____ the total of the debit side should always be equal to the total of the credit side. The _____ thus serves as a tool to detect errors, which can result in the totals not being equal.

   a. Current asset
   b. Depreciation
   c. Trial balance
   d. Bottom line

21. In vector calculus, _____ is a vector differential operator represented by the nabla symbol: ∇.

   _____ is a mathematical tool serving primarily as a convention for mathematical notation; it makes many equations easier to comprehend, write, and remember. Depending on the way _____ is applied, it can describe the gradient (slope), divergence (degree to which something converges or diverges) or curl (rotational motion at points in a fluid.)

   a. BMC Software, Inc.
   b. 3M Company
   c. BNSF Railway
   d. Del

22. The _____, sometimes known as the nominal ledger, is the main accounting record of a business which uses double-entry bookkeeping. It will usually include accounts for such items as current assets, fixed assets, liabilities, revenue and expense items, gains and losses.

The _____ is a collection of the group of accounts that supports the items shown in the major financial statements.

   a. General journal
   b. Sales journal
   c. General ledger
   d. Journal entry

23. In financial accounting, a _____ or statement of financial position is a summary of a person's or organization's balances. Assets, liabilities and ownership equity are listed as of a specific date, such as the end of its financial year. A _____ is often described as a snapshot of a company's financial condition.
   a. Statement of retained earnings
   b. 3M Company
   c. Financial statements
   d. Balance sheet

24. _____ is a company's financial statement that indicates how the revenue is transformed into the net income The purpose of the _____ is to show managers and investors whether the company made or lost money during the period being reported.

The important thing to remember about an _____ is that it represents a period of time.

   a. Income statement
   b. AMEX
   c. AIG
   d. ABC Television Network

25. In financial accounting, a _____ or Statement of cash flows is a financial statement that shows a company's flow of cash. The money coming into the business is called cash inflow, and money going out from the business is called cash outflow. The statement shows how changes in balance sheet and income accounts affect cash and cash equivalents, and breaks the analysis down to operating, investing, and financing activities.

Chapter 3. The Mechanics of Accounting 33

a. BMC Software, Inc.
b. 3M Company
c. BNSF Railway
d. Cash flow statement

26. _____ is the balance of the amounts of cash being received and paid by a business during a defined period of time, sometimes tied to a specific project. Measurement of _____ can be used

- to evaluate the state or performance of a business or project.
- to determine problems with liquidity. Being profitable does not necessarily mean being liquid. A company can fail because of a shortage of cash, even while profitable.
- to project rate of returns. The time of _____s into and out of projects are used as inputs to financial models such as internal rate of return, and net present value.
- to examine income or growth of a business when it is believed that accrual accounting concepts do not represent economic realities. Alternately, _____ can be used to 'validate' the net income generated by accrual accounting.

_____ as a generic term may be used differently depending on context, and certain _____ definitions may be adapted by analysts and users for their own uses. Common terms include operating _____ and free _____.

a. Flow-through entity
b. Controlling interest
c. Cash flow
d. Commercial paper

Chapter 4. Completing the Accounting Cycle

1. Employment is a contract between two parties, one being the employer and the other being the _____. An _____ may be defined as: 'A person in the service of another under any contract of hire, express or implied, oral or written, where the employer has the power or right to control and direct the _____ in the material details of how the work is to be performed.' Black's Law Dictionary page 471 (5th ed. 1979.)
    a. Employee
    b. AIG
    c. AMEX
    d. ABC Television Network

2. _____ of something is, in finance, the adding together of interest or different investments over a period of time such as atoms (1 - the act or process of accruing; 2 - the amount that accrues.) It holds specific meanings in accounting and payroll.

   _____, in accounting, describes the accounting method known as _____ basis, whereby revenues and expenses are recognized when they are accrued, i.e. accumulated (earned or incurred), regardless when the actual cash is received or paid out.

    a. Assets
    b. Earnings before interest, taxes, depreciation and amortization
    c. Accounts receivable
    d. Accrual

3. _____ is a method of accounting whereby economic activities (rather than cash flow) of financial events are considered, because of two complementary principles, which (together) determine the point, at which expenses and revenues are recognized. According to revenue recognition principle, revenues are realized when earned, whether or not they are received in cash.
    a. Earnings before interest, taxes, depreciation and amortization
    b. Accrued revenue
    c. Accrual
    d. Accrual basis accounting

4. According to the Gregorian calendar, the _____ begins on January 1 and ends on December 31.

Generally speaking, a _____ begins on the New Year's Day of the given calendar system and ends on the day before the following New Year's Day. In the Gregorian calendar, this is normally 365 days, but 366 days in a leap year, giving an average length of 365.2425 days.

a. BMC Software, Inc.
b. BNSF Railway
c. 3M Company
d. Calendar year

5. _____ is an acronym for First In, First Out, an abstraction in ways of organizing and manipulation of data relative to time and prioritization. This expression describes the principle of a queue processing technique or servicing conflicting demands by ordering process by first-come, first-served (FCFS) behaviour: what comes in first is handled first, what comes in next waits until the first is finished, etc.

Thus it is analogous to the behaviour of persons queueing (or 'standing in line', in common American parlance), where the persons leave the queue in the order they arrive, or waiting one's turn at a traffic control signal.

a. Risk management
b. Trademark
c. Kanban
d. FIFO

6. The term _____ refers to government debt, expenditures and revenues, or to finance (particularly financial revenue) in general.

- _____ deficit is the budget deficit of federal or local government
- _____ policy is the discretionary spending of governments. Contrasts with monetary policy.
- _____ year and _____ quarter are reporting periods for firms and other agencies.

See also

- Procurator _____ and Crown Office and Procurator _____ Service

a. Scientific Research and Experimental Development Tax Incentive Program
b. Swap
c. Comparable
d. Fiscal

7. _____ is a cornerstone of accrual accounting together with the revenue recognition principle. They both determine the accounting period, in which revenues and expenses are recognized. According to the principle, expenses are recognized when obligations are (1) incurred (usually when goods are transferred or services rendered, e.g. sold), and (2) offset against recognized revenues, which were generated from those expenses (related on the cause-and-effect basis), no matter when cash is paid out.

a. Payroll
b. Matching principle
c. Net sales
d. Current liabilities

8. _____ principle is a cornerstone of accrual accounting together with matching principle. They both determine the accounting period, in which revenues and expenses are recognized. According to the principle, revenues are recognized when they are (1) realized or realizable, and are (2) earned (usually when goods are transferred or services rendered), no matter when cash is received.
   a. 3M Company
   b. BMC Software, Inc.
   c. Net realizable value
   d. Revenue recognition

9. _____ is a method of accounting whereby cash flow of financial events is considered. The method recognizes revenues when cash is received and recognizes expenses when cash is paid out. In cash accounting, revenues and expenses are also called cash receipts and cash payments respectively.
   a. Treasury stock
   b. Net sales
   c. Closing entries
   d. Cash basis accounting

10. In financial accounting, a _____ or Statement of cash flows is a financial statement that shows a company's flow of cash. The money coming into the business is called cash inflow, and money going out from the business is called cash outflow. The statement shows how changes in balance sheet and income accounts affect cash and cash equivalents, and breaks the analysis down to operating, investing, and financing activities.
    a. 3M Company
    b. Cash flow statement
    c. BNSF Railway
    d. BMC Software, Inc.

Chapter 4. Completing the Accounting Cycle

11. _____ is the balance of the amounts of cash being received and paid by a business during a defined period of time, sometimes tied to a specific project. Measurement of _____ can be used

  • to evaluate the state or performance of a business or project.
  • to determine problems with liquidity. Being profitable does not necessarily mean being liquid. A company can fail because of a shortage of cash, even while profitable.
  • to project rate of returns. The time of _____s into and out of projects are used as inputs to financial models such as internal rate of return, and net present value.
  • to examine income or growth of a business when it is believed that accrual accounting concepts do not represent economic realities. Alternately, _____ can be used to 'validate' the net income generated by accrual accounting.

_____ as a generic term may be used differently depending on context, and certain _____ definitions may be adapted by analysts and users for their own uses. Common terms include operating _____ and free _____.

   a. Commercial paper
   b. Controlling interest
   c. Cash flow
   d. Flow-through entity

12. In accounting/accountancy, _____ are journal entries usually made at the end of an accounting period to allocate income and expenditure to the period in which they actually occurred. The revenue recognition principle is the basis of making _____ that pertain to unearned and accrued revenues under accrual-basis accounting. They are sometimes called Balance Day adjustments because they are made on balance day.
   a. Earnings before interest, taxes, depreciation and amortization
   b. Accrual
   c. Adjusting entries
   d. Accrued expense

13. In financial accounting, a _____ is defined as an obligation of an entity arising from past transactions or events, the settlement of which may result in the transfer or use of assets, provision of services or other yielding of economic benefits in the future.
   a. False Claims Act
   b. Corporate governance
   c. Vested
   d. Liability

14. _____ refers to services paid for in advance. Examples include tolls, pay as you go cell phones, and stored-value cards such as gift cards and preloaded credit cards. _____ accounts are assets, and they are increased by debiting the account(s.)

a. BNSF Railway
b. Prepaid
c. 3M Company
d. BMC Software, Inc.

15. _____, in accrual accounting, is any account where the asset or liability is not realized until a future date (accounting period), e.g. annuities, charges, taxes, income, etc. The _____ item may be carried, dependent on type of deferral, as either an asset or liability.
   a. Cash basis accounting
   b. Pro forma
   c. Deferred
   d. Payroll

16. In financial accounting and finance, _____ is the portion of receivables that can no longer be collected, typically from accounts receivable or loans. _____ in accounting is considered an expense.

There are two methods to account for _____:

1. Direct write off method (Non - GAAP)

A receivable which is not considered collectible is charged directly to the income statement.

1. Allowance method (GAAP)

An estimate is made at the end of each fiscal year of the amount of _____. This is then accumulated in a provision which is then used to reduce specific receivable accounts as and when necessary.

   a. Total Expense Ratio
   b. 3M Company
   c. Bad debt
   d. Tax expense

17. _____ is that which is owed; usually referencing assets owed, but the term can also cover moral obligations and other interactions not requiring money. In the case of assets, _____ is a means of using future purchasing power in the present before a summation has been earned. Some companies and corporations use _____ as a part of their overall corporate finance strategy.

Chapter 4. Completing the Accounting Cycle 39

a. Debenture
b. Lender
c. Debt
d. Loan

18. In accounting, _____ has a very specific meaning. It is an outflow of cash or other valuable assets from a person or company to another person or company. This outflow of cash is generally one side of a trade for products or services that have equal or better current or future value to the buyer than to the seller.

a. AIG
b. ABC Television Network
c. AMEX
d. Expense

19. _____, in accrual accounting, (e.g. advance payment received from a client) is, according to revenue recognition, revenue not earned until the delivery of goods or services, which until then, is still owed to the payer, hence remaining a liability.

_____, sometimes referred to as deferred revenue or unearned revenue, shares characteristics with accrued expense with the difference that a liability to be covered latter is cash received FROM a counterpart, while goods or services are to be delivered in a latter period, when such income item is earned, the related revenue item is recognized, and the same amount is deducted from deferred revenues.

a. Matching principle
b. Gross sales
c. Treasury stock
d. Deferred income

20. In accounting, the _____ is a worksheet listing the balance at a certain date, of each ledger account in two columns, namely debit and credit. Under the double-entry system, in any transaction the total of any debits must equal the total of any credits, so in a _____ the total of the debit side should always be equal to the total of the credit side. The _____ thus serves as a tool to detect errors, which can result in the totals not being equal.

a. Trial balance
b. Bottom line
c. Depreciation
d. Current asset

21. In vector calculus, _____ is a vector differential operator represented by the nabla symbol: ∇.

_____ is a mathematical tool serving primarily as a convention for mathematical notation; it makes many equations easier to comprehend, write, and remember. Depending on the way _____ is applied, it can describe the gradient (slope), divergence (degree to which something converges or diverges) or curl (rotational motion at points in a fluid.)

  a. BNSF Railway
  b. BMC Software, Inc.
  c. 3M Company
  d. Del

22. In financial accounting, a _____ or statement of financial position is a summary of a person's or organization's balances. Assets, liabilities and ownership equity are listed as of a specific date, such as the end of its financial year. A _____ is often described as a snapshot of a company's financial condition.

  a. Statement of retained earnings
  b. 3M Company
  c. Financial statements
  d. Balance sheet

23. _____ is a company's financial statement that indicates how the revenue is transformed into the net income The purpose of the _____ is to show managers and investors whether the company made or lost money during the period being reported.

The important thing to remember about an _____ is that it represents a period of time.

  a. AIG
  b. AMEX
  c. ABC Television Network
  d. Income statement

24. The general definition of an _____ is an evaluation of a person, organization, system, process, project or product. _____s are performed to ascertain the validity and reliability of information; also to provide an assessment of a system's internal control. The goal of an _____ is to express an opinion on the person/organization/system (etc) in question, under evaluation based on work done on a test basis.

  a. Audit regime
  b. Assurance service
  c. Institute of Chartered Accountants of India
  d. Audit

Chapter 4. Completing the Accounting Cycle

25. In economics, the _____, (or _____) measures the payments that flow between any individual country and all other countries. It is used to summarize all international economic transactions for that country during a specific time period, usually a year. The _____ is determined by the country's exports and imports of goods, services, and financial capital, as well as financial transfers.
    a. Balance of payments
    b. Moving average
    c. Yield to maturity
    d. Stock split

26. _____ is the recording of the value of assets, liabilities, income, and expenses in the daybooks, journals, and ledgers, in which debit and credit entries are chronologically posted to record changes in value. _____ is often mistaken for accounting, which is the system of recording, verifying, and reporting such information. Practitioners of accounting are called accountants.
    a. Bookkeeping
    b. Debit and credit
    c. Double-entry bookkeeping
    d. Controlling account

27. _____ are journal entries made at the end of an accounting period to transfer temporary accounts to permanent accounts. An 'income summary' account may be used to show the balance between revenue and expenses, or they could be directly closed against retained earnings where dividend payments will be deducted from. This process is used to reset the balance of these temporary accounts to zero for the next accounting period.
    a. Closing entries
    b. Treasury stock
    c. FIFO and LIFO accounting
    d. Trial balance

28. An _____ invented by esteemed professor Karen Osterheld is the system of records a business keeps to maintain its accounting system. This includes the purchase, sales, and other financial processes of the business. The purpose of an _____ is to accumulate data and provide decision makers (investors, creditors, and managers) with information to make decision While this was previously a paper-based process, most modern businesses now use accounting software such as UBS, MYOB etc.
    a. ABC Television Network
    b. AIG
    c. AMEX
    d. Accounting information system

Chapter 5. Introduction to Financial Statement Analysis

1. _____ of a business involves analyzing its financial statements and health, its management and competitive advantages, and its competitors and markets. The term is used to distinguish such analysis from other types of investment analysis, such as quantitative analysis and technical analysis.

    _____ is performed on historical and present data, but with the goal of making financial forecasts.

    a. Fundamental analysis
    b. 3M Company
    c. BNSF Railway
    d. BMC Software, Inc.

2. _____ in economics and business is the result of an exchange and from that trade we assign a numerical monetary value to a good, service or asset. If Alice trades Bob 4 apples for an orange, the _____ of an orange is 4 apples. Inversely, the _____ of an apple is 1/4 oranges.
    a. Price discrimination
    b. Discounts and allowances
    c. Transactional Net Margin Method
    d. Price

3. In finance, a _____ or accounting ratio is a ratio of two selected numerical values taken from an enterprise's financial statements. There are many standard ratios used to try to evaluate the overall financial condition of a corporation or other organization. _____s may be used by managers within a firm, by current and potential shareholders (owners) of a firm, and by a firm's creditors.
    a. Return of capital
    b. Price/cash flow ratio
    c. Current ratio
    d. Financial ratio

4. _____ is that which is owed; usually referencing assets owed, but the term can also cover moral obligations and other interactions not requiring money. In the case of assets, _____ is a means of using future purchasing power in the present before a summation has been earned. Some companies and corporations use _____ as a part of their overall corporate finance strategy.
    a. Debt
    b. Lender
    c. Debenture
    d. Loan

Chapter 5. Introduction to Financial Statement Analysis

5. _____ is a financial ratio that indicates the percentage of a company's assets are provided via debt. It is the ratio of total debt (the sum of current liabilities and long-term liabilities) and total assets (the sum of current assets, fixed assets, and other assets such as 'goodwill'.)

$$\text{Debt ratio} = \frac{\text{Total Debt}}{\text{Total Assets}}$$

or alternatively:

$$\text{Debt ratio} = \frac{\text{Total Liability}}{\text{Total Assets}}$$

For example, a company with $2 million in total assets and $500,000 in total liabilities would have a _____ of 25%

Like all financial ratios, a company's _____ should be compared with their industry average or other competing firms.

   a. Finance lease
   b. Debt ratio
   c. 3M Company
   d. Profitability index

6. A _____ is any one of a variety of different systems, institutions, procedures, social relations and infrastructures whereby persons trade, and goods and services are exchanged, forming part of the economy. It is an arrangement that allows buyers and sellers to exchange things. _____s vary in size, range, geographic scale, location, types and variety of human communities, as well as the types of goods and services traded.
   a. Market
   b. Market Failure
   c. Recession
   d. Perfect competition

7. The _____ is a financial ratio that measures whether or not a firm has enough resources to pay its debts over the next 12 months. It compares a firm's current assets to its current liabilities. It is expressed as follows:

$$\text{Current ratio} = \frac{\text{Current Assets}}{\text{Current Liabilities}}$$

For example, if WXY Company's current assets are $50,000,000 and its current liabilities are $40,000,000, then its _____ would be $50,000,000 divided by $40,000,000, which equals 1.25.

a. Current ratio
b. Return on capital
c. Net Interest Income
d. Times interest earned

8. _____ is a business, economics or investment term that refers to an asset's ability to be easily converted through an act of buying or selling without causing a significant movement in the price and with minimum loss of value. Money, or cash on hand, is the most liquid asset. An act of exchange of a less liquid asset with a more liquid asset is called liquidation.
   a. Financial instruments
   b. Transfer agent
   c. Spot rate
   d. Market liquidity

9. In business and accounting, _____ are everything of value that is owned by a person or company. It is a claim on the property your income of a borrower. The balance sheet of a firm records the monetary value of the _____ owned by the firm.
   a. Earnings before interest, taxes, depreciation and amortization
   b. Assets
   c. Accrual basis accounting
   d. Accounts receivable

10. _____ is a financial ratio that measures the efficiency of a company's use of its assets in generating sales revenue or sales income to the company.

$$Asset\ Turnover = \frac{Sales}{Average\ Total\ Assets}$$

- 'Sales' is the value of 'Net Sales' or 'Sales' from the company's income statement
- 'Average Total Assets' is the value of 'Total assets' from the company's balance sheet in the beginning and the end of the fiscal period divided by 2.

a. Information ratio
b. Enterprise Value/Sales
c. Average propensity to consume
d. Asset turnover

11. _____ measures the rate of return on the ownership interest (shareholders' equity) of the common stock owners. It measures a firm's efficiency at generating profits from every dollar of shareholders' equity (also known as net assets or assets minus liabilities.) It shows how well a company uses investment dollars to generate earnings growth.

   a. Return on equity
   b. Return on capital employed
   c. Sortino ratio
   d. Like for like

12. In business, operating margin, operating income margin, operating profit margin or _____ is the ratio of operating income (operating profit in the UK) divided by net sales, usually presented in percent.

$$\text{Operating margin} = \left(\frac{\text{Operating income}}{\text{Revenue}}\right)$$

(Relevant figures in italics)

$$\text{Operating margin} = \left(\frac{6,318}{24,088}\right) = \underline{\underline{26.23\%}}$$

It is a measurement of what proportion of a company's revenue is left over, before taxes and other indirect costs (such as rent, bonus, interest, etc.), after paying for variable costs of production as wages, raw materials, etc. A good operating margin is needed for a company to be able to pay for its fixed costs, such as interest on debt.

   a. Total revenue share
   b. Debt service coverage ratio
   c. Diluted Earnings Per Share
   d. Return on sales

13. A _____ is the pinnacle activity involved in selling products or services in return for money or other compensation. It is an act of completion of a commercial activity.

A _____ is completed by the seller, the owner of the goods.

   a. High yield stock
   b. Tertiary sector of economy
   c. Sale
   d. Maturity

Chapter 5. Introduction to Financial Statement Analysis

14. _____ is one of a series of accounting transactions dealing with the billing of customers who owe money to a person, company or organization for goods and services that have been provided to the customer. In most business entities this is typically done by generating an invoice and mailing or electronically delivering it to the customer, who in turn must pay it within an established timeframe called credit or payment terms.

An example of a common payment term is Net 30, meaning payment is due in the amount of the invoice 30 days from the date of invoice.

a. Adjusting entries
b. Accrual
c. Accrued revenue
d. Accounts receivable

15. The Exxon Mobil Corporation is an American oil and gas corporation. It is a direct descendant of John D. Rockefeller's Standard Oil company, formed on November 30, 1999, by the merger of Exxon and Mobil.

_____ is the world's largest publicly traded company when measured by either revenue or market capitalization.

a. Abby Joseph Cohen
b. ExxonMobil
c. Arthur Betz Laffer
d. Alan Greenspan

16. _____ are formal records of a business' financial activities.

In British English, including United Kingdom company law, _____ are often referred to as accounts, although the term _____ is also used, particularly by accountants.

_____ provide an overview of a business' financial condition in both short and long term.

a. 3M Company
b. Notes to the financial statements
c. Statement of retained earnings
d. Financial statements

17. _____ is a company's financial statement that indicates how the revenue is transformed into the net income The purpose of the _____ is to show managers and investors whether the company made or lost money during the period being reported.

Chapter 5. Introduction to Financial Statement Analysis 47

The important thing to remember about an _____ is that it represents a period of time.

a. AMEX
b. ABC Television Network
c. Income statement
d. AIG

18. In financial accounting, a _____ or statement of financial position is a summary of a person's or organization's balances. Assets, liabilities and ownership equity are listed as of a specific date, such as the end of its financial year. A _____ is often described as a snapshot of a company's financial condition.

a. Statement of retained earnings
b. Financial statements
c. 3M Company
d. Balance sheet

19. The _____, a ratio that is typically applied to banks, in simple terms is defined as expenses as a percentage of revenue (expenses / revenue), with a few variations. A lower percentage is better since that means expenses are low and earnings are high. It is related to operating leverage, which measures the ratio between fixed costs and variable costs.

a. Equity ratio
b. Efficiency ratio
c. Operating leverage
d. Average rate of return

20. _____ is the balance of the amounts of cash being received and paid by a business during a defined period of time, sometimes tied to a specific project. Measurement of _____ can be used

- to evaluate the state or performance of a business or project.
- to determine problems with liquidity. Being profitable does not necessarily mean being liquid. A company can fail because of a shortage of cash, even while profitable.
- to project rate of returns. The time of _____s into and out of projects are used as inputs to financial models such as internal rate of return, and net present value.
- to examine income or growth of a business when it is believed that accrual accounting concepts do not represent economic realities. Alternately, _____ can be used to 'validate' the net income generated by accrual accounting.

_____ as a generic term may be used differently depending on context, and certain _____ definitions may be adapted by analysts and users for their own uses. Common terms include operating _____ and free _____.

Chapter 5. Introduction to Financial Statement Analysis

a. Controlling interest
b. Flow-through entity
c. Commercial paper
d. Cash flow

21. In financial accounting and finance, _____ is the portion of receivables that can no longer be collected, typically from accounts receivable or loans. _____ in accounting is considered an expense.

There are two methods to account for _____:

1. Direct write off method (Non - GAAP)

A receivable which is not considered collectible is charged directly to the income statement.

1. Allowance method (GAAP)

An estimate is made at the end of each fiscal year of the amount of _____. This is then accumulated in a provision which is then used to reduce specific receivable accounts as and when necessary.

a. Tax expense
b. 3M Company
c. Total Expense Ratio
d. Bad debt

22. In accounting, _____ has a very specific meaning. It is an outflow of cash or other valuable assets from a person or company to another person or company. This outflow of cash is generally one side of a trade for products or services that have equal or better current or future value to the buyer than to the seller.

a. AIG
b. ABC Television Network
c. AMEX
d. Expense

23. _____, also referred to simply as a 'public offering' or 'flotation,' is when a company issues common stock or shares to the public for the first time. They are often issued by smaller, younger companies seeking capital to expand, but can also be done by large privately-owned companies looking to become publicly traded.

In an _____ the issuer may obtain the assistance of an underwriting firm, which helps it determine what type of security to issue (common or preferred), best offering price and time to bring it to market.

Chapter 5. Introduction to Financial Statement Analysis

a. Intergenerational equity
b. Insolvency
c. AT'T Wireless Services, Inc.
d. Initial public offering

24. A _____ is a type of debt Like all debt instruments, a _____ entails the redistribution of financial assets over time, between the lender and the borrower.

a. Lender
b. Loan to value
c. Loan
d. Debenture

25. _____ is equal to the income that a firm has after subtracting costs and expenses from the total revenue. _____ can be distributed among holders of common stock as a dividend or held by the firm as retained earnings.

The items deducted will typically include tax expense, financing expense (interest expense), and minority interest. Likewise, preferred stock dividends will be subtracted too, though they are not an expense.

a. Net income
b. Generally accepted accounting principles
c. Long-term liabilities
d. Matching principle

26. In mathematics, two elements x and y of a set partially ordered by a relation ≤ are said to be _____ if and only if x ≤ y or y ≤ x if and only if x < y or y < x or y = x. For example, two sets are _____ with respect to inclusion if and only if one is a subset of the other.

In a classification of mathematical objects such as topological spaces, two criteria are said to be _____ when the objects that obey one criterion constitute a subset of the objects that obey the other one.

a. Consumption
b. Database auditing
c. Comparable
d. Scientific Research and Experimental Development Tax Incentive Program

Chapter 6. Ensuring the Integrity of Financial Information

1. In the technical language of the World Trade Organization (WTO) system, a _____ is used to restrain international trade in order to protect a certain home industry from foreign competition. A member may take a e;_____e; action (i.e., restrict importation of a product temporarily) to protect a specific domestic industry from an increase in imports of any product which is causing, or which is threatening to cause, serious injury to the domestic industry that produces like or directly-competitive products.

    _____ measures were always available under the General Agreement on Tariffs and Trade (GATT) (Article XIX.)

    a. 3M Company
    b. BNSF Railway
    c. BMC Software, Inc.
    d. Safeguard

2. In economics, the _____, (or _____) measures the payments that flow between any individual country and all other countries. It is used to summarize all international economic transactions for that country during a specific time period, usually a year. The _____ is determined by the country's exports and imports of goods, services, and financial capital, as well as financial transfers.
    a. Moving average
    b. Stock split
    c. Yield to maturity
    d. Balance of payments

3. A _____ has several related meanings:

    - a daily record of events or business; a private _____ is usually referred to as a diary.
    - a newspaper or other periodical, in the literal sense of one published each day;
    - many publications issued at stated intervals, such as magazines, or scholarly academic _____s, or the record of the transactions of a society, are often called _____s. Although _____ is sometimes used, erroneously, as a synonym for 'magazine,' in academic use, a _____ refers to a serious, scholarly publication, most often peer-reviewed. A non-scholarly magazine written for an educated audience about an industry or an area of professional activity is usually called a professional magazine.

The word 'journalist' for one whose business is writing for the public press has been in use since the end of the 17th century.

Open access _____s are scholarly _____s that are available to the reader without financial or other barrier other than access to the internet itself. Some are subsidized, and some require payment on behalf of the author. Subsidized _____s are financed by an academic institution or a government information center.

Chapter 6. Ensuring the Integrity of Financial Information

a. BNSF Railway
b. 3M Company
c. Journal
d. BMC Software, Inc.

4. The basic _____ is the foundation for the double-entry bookkeeping system. It shows how assets were financed: either by borrowing money from someone (liability) or by paying your own money (shareholders' equity.)

   Assets = Liabilities + (Shareholders or Owners equity)

For example: A student buys a computer for $945.

a. AIG
b. ABC Television Network
c. AMEX
d. Accounting equation

5. An _____ is a practitioner of accountancy, which is the measurement, disclosure or provision of assurance about financial information that helps managers, investors, tax authorities and other decision makers make resource allocation decisions.

The word '_____' is derived from the French 'Compter' which took its origin from the Latin 'Computare'. The word was formerly written in English as 'Accomptant', but in process of time the word, which was always pronounced by dropping the 'p', became gradually changed both in pronunciation and in orthography to its present form.

a. AIG
b. AMEX
c. Accountant
d. ABC Television Network

6. The _____ is the national, professional association of CPAs in the United States, with more than 330,000 members, including CPAs in business and industry, public practice, government, and education; student affiliates; and international associates. It sets ethical standards for the profession and U.S. auditing standards for audits of private companies; federal, state and local governments; and non-profit organizations.

Approximately 40% of its members are engaged in the practice of public accounting, in areas such as auditing, accounting, taxation, general business consulting, business valuation, personal financial planning and business technology.

a. ABC Television Network
b. Other postemployment benefits
c. AIG
d. American Institute of Certified Public Accountants

7. _____ is the statutory title of qualified accountants in the United States who have passed the Uniform _____ Examination and have met additional state education and experience requirements for certification as a _____. Individuals who have passed the Exam but have not either accomplished the required on-the-job experience or have previously met it but in the meantime have lapsed their continuing professional education are, in many states, permitted the designation '_____ Inactive' or an equivalent phrase. In most U.S. states, only _____s who are licensed are able to provide to the public attestation (including auditing) opinions on financial statements.
 a. Certified Public Accountant
 b. Chartered Certified Accountant
 c. Certified General Accountant
 d. Chartered Accountant

8. An _____ is a term used in behavioral economics to describe those types of behaviors that impose costs on a person in the long-run that are not taken into account when making decisions in the present. Classical Economics discourages government from creating legislation that targets internalities, because it is assumed that the consumer takes these personal costs into account when paying for the good that causes the _____. For example, cigarettes should be taxed because of the negative consumption externalities that they impose, such as second-hand smoke, not because the smoker harms him or herself by smoking.
 a. Authorised capital
 b. Internality
 c. Inventory turnover ratio
 d. Operating budget

9. In accounting and organizational theory, _____ is defined as a process effected by an organization's structure, work and authority flows, people and management information systems, designed to help the organization accomplish specific goals or objectives. It is a means by which an organization's resources are directed, monitored, and measured. It plays an important role in preventing and detecting fraud and protecting the organization's resources, both physical (e.g., machinery and property) and intangible (e.g., reputation or intellectual property such as trademarks.)
 a. Internal control
 b. Auditor independence
 c. Audit risk
 d. Audit committee

Chapter 6. Ensuring the Integrity of Financial Information

10. _____ also called 'Internal _____'. It is a term of financial audit, internal audit and Enterprise Risk Management. It means the overall attitude, awareness and actions of directors and management (i.e. 'those charged with governance') regarding the internal control system and its importance to the entity.

   a. Negative assurance
   b. Mainframe audit
   c. SOFT audit
   d. Control environment

11. The _____ of 1977 (15 U.S.C. §§ 78dd-1, et seq.) is a United States federal law known primarily for two of its main provisions, one that addresses accounting transparency requirements under the Securities Exchange Act of 1934 and another concerning bribery of foreign officials.

   a. Competition law
   b. Lease
   c. Pre-emption right
   d. Foreign Corrupt Practices Act

12. The _____ is the current method of accelerated asset depreciation required by the United States income tax code. Under _____, all assets are divided into classes which dictate the number of years over which an asset's cost will be recovered.

   Prior to the Accelerated Cost Recovery System (ACRS), most capital purchases were depreciated using a straight line technique, that allowed for the depreciation of the asset over its useful life.

   a. BMC Software, Inc.
   b. 3M Company
   c. Categorical grants
   d. Modified Accelerated Cost Recovery System

13. The _____ of 2002 (Pub.L. 107-204, 116 Stat. 745, enacted July 30, 2002), also known as the Public Company Accounting Reform and Investor Protection Act of 2002, is a United States federal law enacted on July 30, 2002 in response to a number of major corporate and accounting scandals including those affecting Enron, Tyco International, Adelphia, Peregrine Systems and WorldCom. The legislation establishes new or enhanced standards for all U.S. public company boards, management, and public accounting firms. It does not apply to privately held companies.

   a. FCPA
   b. Lease
   c. Sarbanes-Oxley Act
   d. Fair Labor Standards Act

Chapter 6. Ensuring the Integrity of Financial Information

14. The general definition of an _____ is an evaluation of a person, organization, system, process, project or product. _____s are performed to ascertain the validity and reliability of information; also to provide an assessment of a system's internal control. The goal of an _____ is to express an opinion on the person/organization/system (etc) in question, under evaluation based on work done on a test basis.

   a. Assurance service
   b. Institute of Chartered Accountants of India
   c. Audit regime
   d. Audit

15. An _____ is a mostly hierarchical concept of subordination of entities that collaborate and contribute to serve one common aim.

Organizations are a variant of clustered entities. The structure of an organization is usually set up in many a styles, dependent on their objectives and ambience.

   a. AMEX
   b. AIG
   c. ABC Television Network
   d. Organizational structure

16. _____ is the concept of having more than one person required to complete a task. It is alternatively called segregation of duties or, in the political realm, separation of powers.

_____ is one of the key concepts of internal control and is the most difficult and sometimes the most costly one to achieve. The term _____ is already well-known in financial accounting systems. Companies in all sizes understand not to combine roles such as receiving checks (payment on account) and approving write-offs, depositing cash and reconciling bank statements, approving time cards and have custody of pay checks, etc.

   a. 3M Company
   b. BMC Software, Inc.
   c. Separation of duties
   d. Salary

17. In business and accounting, _____ are everything of value that is owned by a person or company. It is a claim on the property your income of a borrower. The balance sheet of a firm records the monetary value of the _____ owned by the firm.

Chapter 6. Ensuring the Integrity of Financial Information

a. Accounts receivable
b. Accrual basis accounting
c. Earnings before interest, taxes, depreciation and amortization
d. Assets

18. _____ is a specific term used in companies' financial reporting from the company-whole point of view. Because that use excludes the effects of changing ownership interest, an economic measure of _____ is necessary for financial analysis from the shareholders' point of view

_____ is defined by the Financial Accounting Standards Board, or FASB, as 'the change in equity [net assets] of a business enterprise during a period from transactions and other events and circumstances from nonowner sources. It includes all changes in equity during a period except those resulting from investments by owners and distributions to owners.'

_____ is the sum of net income and other items that must bypass the income statement because they have not been realized, including items like an unrealized holding gain or loss from available for sale securities and foreign currency translation gains or losses.

a. BMC Software, Inc.
b. BNSF Railway
c. 3M Company
d. Comprehensive income

19. Creative accounting and _____ are euphemisms referring to accounting practices that may follow the letter of the rules of standard accounting practices, but certainly deviate from the spirit of those rules. They are characterized by excessive complication and the use of novel ways of characterizing income, assets, or liabilities and the intent to influence readers towards the interpretations desired by the authors. The terms 'innovative' or 'aggressive' are also sometimes used.
a. ABC Television Network
b. AMEX
c. AIG
d. Earnings management

20. _____ is a process by which a firm can obtain the use of a certain fixed assets for which it must pay a series of contractual, periodic, tax deductable payments. The lessee is the receiver of the services or the assets under the lease contract and the lessor is the owner of the assets. The relationship between the tenant and the landlord is called a tenancy, and can be for a fixed or an indefinite period of time (called the term of the lease.)

Chapter 6. Ensuring the Integrity of Financial Information

a. Resource Conservation and Recovery Act
b. Federal Sentencing Guidelines
c. Leasing
d. Property

21. _____ means the giving out of information, either voluntarily or to be in compliance with legal regulations or workplace rules.

- In Computer security, full _____ means disclosing full information about vulnerabilities.
- In computing, _____ widget
- Journalism, full _____ refers to disclosing the interests of the writer which may bear on the subject being written about, for example, if the writer has worked with an interview subject in the past.

- In law:
    - The law of England and Wales, _____ refers to a process that may form part of legal proceedings, whereby parties inform to other parties the existence of any relevant documents that are, or have been, in their control. This compares with the process known as discovery in the course of legal proceedings in the United States.
    - In U.S. civil procedure (litigation rules for civil cases), _____ is a stage prior to trial. In civil cases, each party must disclose to the opposing party the following: names of witnesses which it may use to support its side, copies of documents (or mere description of these documents) in its control which it may use to support its side, computation of damages claimed, and certain insurance information. _____ is related to, but technically prior to, the discovery stage.
    - In Company law (known as 'corporate law' in the United States), _____ refers to giving out information about public or limited companies or their officers, which might be kept secret if the company was a private company or a partnership.

- In real property transactions, _____ refers to providing to a buyer information known to the seller or broker/agent concerning the condition or other aspects of real property that would affect the property's value or desirability. These rules regarding what information must be disclosed, and whether the information must be disclosed even if a buyer does not ask, vary from one jurisdiction to the next.

a. Disclosure
b. Trailing
c. Tax harmonisation
d. Controlled Foreign Corporations

22. _____, also referred to simply as a 'public offering' or 'flotation,' is when a company issues common stock or shares to the public for the first time. They are often issued by smaller, younger companies seeking capital to expand, but can also be done by large privately-owned companies looking to become publicly traded.

In an _____ the issuer may obtain the assistance of an underwriting firm, which helps it determine what type of security to issue (common or preferred), best offering price and time to bring it to market.

a. Initial public offering
b. Intergenerational equity
c. AT'T Wireless Services, Inc.
d. Insolvency

23. A _____ is a type of debt Like all debt instruments, a _____ entails the redistribution of financial assets over time, between the lender and the borrower.

a. Debenture
b. Loan to value
c. Lender
d. Loan

24. In computer security, _____ means to disclose all the details of a security problem which are known. It is a philosophy of security management completely opposed to the idea of security through obscurity. The concept of _____ is controversial, but not new; it has been an issue for locksmiths since the 19th century.

a. 3M Company
b. BNSF Railway
c. BMC Software, Inc.
d. Full Disclosure

25. _____ is the term used to refer to the standard framework of guidelines for financial accounting used in any given jurisdiction. _____ includes the standards, conventions, and rules accountants follow in recording and summarizing transactions, and in the preparation of financial statements.

Financial accounting information must be assembled and reported objectively.

a. Current asset
b. Long-term liabilities
c. General ledger
d. Generally accepted accounting principles

26. The term _____ usually refers to a company that is permitted to offer its registered securities (stock, bonds, etc.) for sale to the general public, typically through a stock exchange, or occasionally a company whose stock is traded over the counter (OTC) via market makers who use non-exchange quotation services.

The term '_____' may also refer to a company owned by the government.

  a. Governmental Accounting Standards Board
  b. MicroStrategy
  c. Professional association
  d. Public Company

27. The _____ (sometimes called 'Peekaboo') is a private-sector, non-profit corporation created by the Sarbanes-Oxley Act, a 2002 United States federal law, to oversee the auditors of public companies. Its stated purpose is to 'protect the interests of investors and further the public interest in the preparation of informative, fair, and independent audit reports'. Although a private entity, the _____ has many government-like regulatory functions, making it in some ways similar to the private Self Regulatory Organizations (SROs) that regulate stock markets and other aspects of the financial markets in the United States.
  a. Public Company Accounting Oversight Board
  b. Pension Benefit Guaranty Corporation
  c. 3M Company
  d. Financial Crimes Enforcement Network

28. An _____ is an audit professional who performs an audit on the financial statements of a company, government, individual and who is independent of the entity being audited. Users of these entities' financial information, such as investors, government agencies, and the general public, rely on the _____ to present an unbiased and independent evaluation on such entities. They are distinguished from internal auditors for two main reasons: (1) the internal auditor's primary responsibility is appraising an entity's risk management strategy and practices, management (including IT) control frameworks and governance processes, and (2) they do not express an opinion on the entity's financial statements.
  a. International Federation of Audit Bureaux of Circulations
  b. External auditor
  c. Audit risk
  d. Event data

29. _____ are ten auditing standards, developed by the AICPA, consisting of general standards, standards of field work, and standards of reporting, along with interpretations. They were developed by the AICPA in 1947 and have undergone minor changes since then.

Chapter 6. Ensuring the Integrity of Financial Information 59

The _____ are as follows:

1. The auditor must have adequate technical training and proficiency to perform the audit
2. The auditor must maintain independence in mental attitude in all matters related to the audit.
3. The auditor must use due professional care during the performance of the audit and the preparation of the report.

1. The auditor must adequately plan the work and must properly supervise any assistants.
2. The auditor must obtain a sufficient understanding of the entity and its environment, including its internal control, to assess the risk of material misstatement of the financial statements whether due to error or fraud, and to design the nature, timing, and extent of further audit procedures.
3. The auditor must obtain sufficient appropriate audit evidence by performing audit procedures to afford a reasonable basis for an opinion regarding the financial statements under audit.

The new standards are in effect for audits of financial statements for periods beginning on or after December 15, 2006.

1. The auditor must state in the auditor's report whether the financial statements are in accordance with generally accepted accounting principles (GAAP.)
2. The auditor must identify in the auditor's report those circumstances in which such principles have not been consistently observed in the current period in relation to the preceding period.
3. When the auditor determines that informative disclosures are not reasonably adequate, the auditor must so state in the auditor's report.
4. The auditor must either express an opinion regarding the financial statements, taken as a whole the auditor should state the reasons therefore in the auditor's report. In all cases where the auditor's name is associated with the financial statements, the auditor should clearly indicate the character of the auditor's work, if any, and the degree of responsibility the auditor is taking, in the auditor's report.

a. Generally accepted auditing standards
b. Continuous auditing
c. Negative assurance
d. Joint audit

30. Internal auditing is a profession and activity involved in helping organisations achieve their stated objectives. It does this by utilizing a systematic methodology for analyzing business processes, procedures and activities with the goal of highlighting organizational problems and recommending solutions. Professionals called _____ are employed by organizations to perform the internal auditing activity.

a. Internal auditors
b. Auditor independence
c. Auditing Standards Board
d. Internal Auditing

31. _____ is one of financial audit skill which help an auditor understand the client's business and changes in the business, to identify potential risk areas and to plan other audit procedures.

_____ include comparison of financial information (data in financial statement) with

1. prior periods
2. budgets
3. forecasts
4. similar industries and so on.

It also includes consideration of predictable relationships, such as:

1. gross profit to sales,
2. payroll costs to employees,
3. financial information and non-financial information, for examples the CEO's reports and the industry news.

possible sources of information about the client include:

1. interim financial information
2. Budgets
3. Management accounts
4. Non-Financial information
5. Bank and cash records
6. VAT returns
7. Board minutes
8. Discussion or correspondance with the client at they year-end

a. External auditor
b. International Federation of Audit Bureaux of Circulations
c. Analytical procedures
d. Assurance service

32. A _____ is a fungible, negotiable instrument representing financial value. they are broadly categorized into debt securities (such as banknotes, bonds and debentures), and equity securities; e.g., common stocks. The company or other entity issuing the _____ is called the issuer.

a. Security
b. Tracking stock
c. 3M Company
d. BMC Software, Inc.

33. The U.S. _____ is an independent agency of the United States government which holds primary responsibility for enforcing the federal securities laws and regulating the securities industry, the nation's stock and options exchanges, and other electronic securities markets. The SEC was created by section 4 of the Securities Exchange Act of 1934 (now codified as 15 U.S.C. §§ 78d and commonly referred to as the 1934 Act.)
   a. BMC Software, Inc.
   b. Securities and Exchange Commission
   c. 3M Company
   d. BNSF Railway

34. A _____ is an annual report required by the U.S. Securities and Exchange Commission (SEC), that gives a comprehensive summary of a public company's performance. Although similarly named, the annual report on _____ is distinct from the often glossy 'annual report to shareholders', which a company must send to its shareholders when it holds an annual meeting to elect directors (though some companies combine the annual report and the 10-K into one document.) The 10-K includes information such as company history, organizational structure, executive compensation, equity, subsidiaries, and audited financial statements, among other information.
   a. 3M Company
   b. Form 8-K
   c. Form 10-K
   d. Form 10-Q

35. _____, Quarterly Report Pursuant to Section 13 or 15(d) of the Securities Exchange Act of 1934, is an SEC filing that must be filed quarterly with the US Securities and Exchange Commission. It contains similar information to the annual form 10-K, however the information is generally less detailed, and the financial statements are generally unaudited. Information for the final quarter of a firm's fiscal year is included in the 10-K, so only three 10-Q filings are made each year.
   a. 3M Company
   b. Form 8-K
   c. Form 10-Q
   d. Form 20-F

Chapter 7. Selling a Product or a Service

1. In economics, _____ or _____ goods or real _____ refers to factors of production used to create goods or services that are not themselves significantly consumed (though they may depreciate) in the production process. _____ goods may be acquired with money or financial _____. In finance and accounting, _____ generally refers to financial wealth, especially that used to start or maintain a business.
   a. Disclosure
   b. Capital
   c. Screening
   d. Vyborg Appeal

2. _____ principle is a cornerstone of accrual accounting together with matching principle. They both determine the accounting period, in which revenues and expenses are recognized. According to the principle, revenues are recognized when they are (1) realized or realizable, and are (2) earned (usually when goods are transferred or services rendered), no matter when cash is received.
   a. BMC Software, Inc.
   b. 3M Company
   c. Revenue recognition
   d. Net realizable value

3. A _____ is the pinnacle activity involved in selling products or services in return for money or other compensation. It is an act of completion of a commercial activity.

   A _____ is completed by the seller, the owner of the goods.

   a. Tertiary sector of economy
   b. High yield stock
   c. Sale
   d. Maturity

4. A _____ is a fungible, negotiable instrument representing financial value. they are broadly categorized into debt securities (such as banknotes, bonds and debentures), and equity securities; e.g., common stocks. The company or other entity issuing the _____ is called the issuer.
   a. Security
   b. 3M Company
   c. Tracking stock
   d. BMC Software, Inc.

5. _____ is the state or fact of exclusive rights and control over property, which may be an object, land/real estate or intellectual property. An _____ right is also referred to as title.

Chapter 7. Selling a Product or a Service

_____ is the key building block in the development of the capitalist socio-economic system.

a. Ownership
b. Administrative proceeding
c. Encumbrance
d. ABC Television Network

6. In economics, the _____, (or _____) measures the payments that flow between any individual country and all other countries. It is used to summarize all international economic transactions for that country during a specific time period, usually a year. The _____ is determined by the country's exports and imports of goods, services, and financial capital, as well as financial transfers.
a. Moving average
b. Stock split
c. Yield to maturity
d. Balance of payments

7. _____ are formal bookkeeping and accounting terms. They are the most fundamental concepts in accounting, representing the two records that one party in a transaction makes on its records, transferring a money balance from one account to another, one representing a reduction of liability or increase in asset, and the other representing a balancing increase in liability or reduction of asset.

Debits and credits are a system of notation used in accounting to keep track of money movements (transactions) into and out of an account.

a. Debit and credit
b. Bookkeeping
c. Cookie jar accounting
d. Controlling account

8. Discounting is a financial mechanism in which a debtor obtains the right to delay payments to a creditor, for a defined period of time, in exchange for a charge or fee. Essentially, the party that owes money in the present purchases the right to delay the payment until some future date. The _____, or charge, is simply the difference between the original amount owed in the present and the amount that has to be paid in the future to settle the debt.
a. Risk aversion
b. Discount factor
c. Discount
d. Discounting

9. In finance, a _____ is a debt security, in which the authorized issuer owes the holders a debt and, depending on the terms of the _____, is obliged to pay interest (the coupon) and/or to repay the principal at a later date, termed maturity. It is a formal contract to repay borrowed money with interest at fixed intervals.

Thus a _____ is like a loan: the issuer is the borrower, the _____ holder is the lender, and the coupon is the interest.

   a. Coupon rate
   b. Zero-coupon bond
   c. Revenue bonds
   d. Bond

10. _____ is defined to be the total invoice value of sales, before deducting customers' discounts, returns, or allowances.

   a. Generally accepted accounting principles
   b. Net profit
   c. Current asset
   d. Gross sales

11. In bookkeeping, accounting, and finance, _____ are operating revenues earned by a company when it sells its products. Revenue (_____) are reported directly on the income statement as Sales or _____.

In financial ratios that use income statement sales values, 'sales' refers to _____, not gross sales.

   a. Historical cost
   b. Deferred
   c. Matching principle
   d. Net sales

12. _____ is one of a series of accounting transactions dealing with the billing of customers who owe money to a person, company or organization for goods and services that have been provided to the customer. In most business entities this is typically done by generating an invoice and mailing or electronically delivering it to the customer, who in turn must pay it within an established timeframe called credit or payment terms.

An example of a common payment term is Net 30, meaning payment is due in the amount of the invoice 30 days from the date of invoice.

a. Accrual
b. Adjusting entries
c. Accounts receivable
d. Accrued revenue

13. In financial accounting and finance, _____ is the portion of receivables that can no longer be collected, typically from accounts receivable or loans. _____ in accounting is considered an expense.

There are two methods to account for _____:

1. Direct write off method (Non - GAAP)

A receivable which is not considered collectible is charged directly to the income statement.

1. Allowance method (GAAP)

An estimate is made at the end of each fiscal year of the amount of _____. This is then accumulated in a provision which is then used to reduce specific receivable accounts as and when necessary.

a. Total Expense Ratio
b. Tax expense
c. 3M Company
d. Bad debt

14. _____ is that which is owed; usually referencing assets owed, but the term can also cover moral obligations and other interactions not requiring money. In the case of assets, _____ is a means of using future purchasing power in the present before a summation has been earned. Some companies and corporations use _____ as a part of their overall corporate finance strategy.
a. Lender
b. Loan
c. Debenture
d. Debt

15. A _____, also client, buyer or purchaser is the buyer or user of the paid products of an individual or organization, mostly called the supplier or seller. This is typically through purchasing or renting goods or services.

a. BNSF Railway
b. 3M Company
c. Customer
d. BMC Software, Inc.

16. In accounting, _____ has a very specific meaning. It is an outflow of cash or other valuable assets from a person or company to another person or company. This outflow of cash is generally one side of a trade for products or services that have equal or better current or future value to the buyer than to the seller.
   a. AIG
   b. AMEX
   c. ABC Television Network
   d. Expense

17. The term _____ describes a reduction in recognized value. In accounting terminology, it refers to recognition of the reduced or zero value of an asset. In income tax statements, it refers to a reduction of taxable income as recognition of certain expenses required to produce the income.
   a. Write-off
   b. Current asset
   c. Payroll
   d. Salvage value

18. In vector calculus, _____ is a vector differential operator represented by the nabla symbol: ∇.

_____ is a mathematical tool serving primarily as a convention for mathematical notation; it makes many equations easier to comprehend, write, and remember. Depending on the way _____ is applied, it can describe the gradient (slope), divergence (degree to which something converges or diverges) or curl (rotational motion at points in a fluid.)

   a. BMC Software, Inc.
   b. 3M Company
   c. BNSF Railway
   d. Del

19. _____ is a method of evaluating an asset's worth when held in inventory, in the field of accounting. _____ is part of the Generally Accepted Accounting Principles that apply to valuing inventory, so as to not overstate or understate the value of inventory goods. Net realisable value is generally equal to the selling price of the inventory goods less the selling costs (completion and disposal).

a. BMC Software, Inc.
b. Revenue recognition
c. 3M Company
d. Net realizable value

20. _____ is the calculated approximation of a result which is usable even if input data may be incomplete or uncertain.

In statistics, see _____ theory, estimator.

In mathematics, approximation or _____ typically means finding upper or lower bounds of a quantity that cannot readily be computed precisely and is also an educated guess .

a. ABC Television Network
b. AIG
c. AMEX
d. Estimation

21. In economics, business, retail, and accounting, a _____ is the value of money that has been used up to produce something, and hence is not available for use anymore. In economics, a _____ is an alternative that is given up as a result of a decision. In business, the _____ may be one of acquisition, in which case the amount of money expended to acquire it is counted as _____.
a. Cost
b. Cost of quality
c. Prime cost
d. Cost allocation

22. _____ is the process of matching and comparing figures from accounting records against those presented on a bank statement. Less any items which have no relation to the bank statement, the balance of the accounting ledger should reconcile (match) to the balance of the bank statement.

_____ allows companies or individuals to compare their account records to the bank's records of their account balance in order to uncover any possible discrepancies.

a. Bank reconciliation
b. Lower of Cost or Market
c. Credit memo
d. Bankruptcy prediction

23. An account statement or a _____ is a summary of all financial transactions occurring over a given period of time on a deposit account, a credit card, or any other type of account offered by a financial institution.

_____s are typically printed on one or several pieces of paper and either mailed directly to the account holder's address, or kept at the financial institution's local branch for pick-up. Certain ATMs offer the possibility to print, at any time, a condensed version of a _____.

   a. Bank statement
   b. BMC Software, Inc.
   c. 3M Company
   d. BNSF Railway

24. The basic _____ is the foundation for the double-entry bookkeeping system. It shows how assets were financed: either by borrowing money from someone (liability) or by paying your own money (shareholders' equity.)

   Assets = Liabilities + (Shareholders or Owners equity)

For example: A student buys a computer for $945.

   a. AMEX
   b. AIG
   c. Accounting equation
   d. ABC Television Network

25. In monetary economics _____ can refer either to a particular _____, for example British Pounds or United States Dollars, or, to the coins and banknotes of a particular _____, which actually form only a small part of the monetary base of a nation's money supply. The other part of a nation's money supply consists of money deposited in banks (sometimes called deposit money), ownership of which can be transferred by means of checks (cheques in the United Kingdom and Australia) or other forms of money transfer such as credit and debit cards. Deposit money and _____ are 'money' in the sense that both are acceptable as a means of exchange, but money need not necessarily be '_____'.
   a. Currency
   b. 3M Company
   c. BNSF Railway
   d. BMC Software, Inc.

Chapter 8. Inventory

1. In economics, business, retail, and accounting, a _____ is the value of money that has been used up to produce something, and hence is not available for use anymore. In economics, a _____ is an alternative that is given up as a result of a decision. In business, the _____ may be one of acquisition, in which case the amount of money expended to acquire it is counted as _____.
   a. Cost of quality
   b. Cost allocation
   c. Prime cost
   d. Cost

2. In financial accounting, _____ or cost of sales includes the direct costs attributable to the production of the goods sold by a company. This amount includes the materials cost used in creating the goods along with the direct labor costs used to produce the good. It excludes indirect expenses such as distribution costs and sales force costs.
   a. 3M Company
   b. Reorder point
   c. Cost of goods sold
   d. FIFO and LIFO accounting

3. _____s are goods that have completed the manufacturing process but have not yet been sold or distributed to the end user.

Manufacturing has three classes of inventory:

   1. Raw material
   2. Work in process
   3. _____s

A good purchased as a 'raw material' goes into the manufacture of a product. A good only partially completed during the manufacturing process is called 'work in process'. When the good is completed as to manufacturing but not yet sold or distributed to the end-user is called a '_____'.

   a. FIFO and LIFO accounting
   b. Finished good
   c. Reorder point
   d. 3M Company

4. In business, _____, Overhead cost or _____ expense refers to an ongoing expense of operating a business. The term _____ is usually used to group expenses that are necessary to the continued functioning of the business, but do not directly generate profits.

_____ expenses are all costs on the income statement except for direct labor and direct materials.

Chapter 8. Inventory

a. ABC Television Network
b. AIG
c. Intangible assets
d. Overhead

5. A _____ is something that is acted upon or used by or by human labour or industry, for use as a building material to create some product or structure. Often the term is used to denote material that came from nature and is in an unprocessed or minimally processed state. Iron ore, logs, and crude oil, would be examples.
   a. 3M Company
   b. BMC Software, Inc.
   c. BNSF Railway
   d. Raw material

6. _____ or in-process inventory includes the set at large of unfinished items for products in a production process. These items are not yet completed but either just being fabricated or waiting in a queue for further processing or in a buffer storage. The term is used in production and supply chain management.
   a. BNSF Railway
   b. BMC Software, Inc.
   c. 3M Company
   d. Work in process

7. A _____ is a fungible, negotiable instrument representing financial value. they are broadly categorized into debt securities (such as banknotes, bonds and debentures), and equity securities; e.g., common stocks. The company or other entity issuing the _____ is called the issuer.
   a. Tracking stock
   b. BMC Software, Inc.
   c. Security
   d. 3M Company

8. _____ is the state or fact of exclusive rights and control over property, which may be an object, land/real estate or intellectual property. An _____ right is also referred to as title.

_____ is the key building block in the development of the capitalist socio-economic system.

Chapter 8. Inventory

a. Administrative proceeding
b. Ownership
c. ABC Television Network
d. Encumbrance

9. _____ is the amount of inventory a company have in stock at the end of this fiscal year. It is closely related with _____ Cost, which is the amount of money spent to get these goods in stock. It should be calculated at the Lower of Cost or Market.
   a. Inventory turnover ratio
   b. ABC Television Network
   c. AIG
   d. Ending inventory

10. A _____ is the pinnacle activity involved in selling products or services in return for money or other compensation. It is an act of completion of a commercial activity.

A _____ is completed by the seller, the owner of the goods.

   a. High yield stock
   b. Sale
   c. Maturity
   d. Tertiary sector of economy

11. _____ refers to a business or organization attempting to acquire goods or services to accomplish the goals of the enterprise. Though there are several organizations that attempt to set standards in the _____ process, processes can vary greatly between organizations. Typically the word e;_____e; is not used interchangeably with the word e;procuremente;, since procurement typically includes Expediting, Supplier Quality, and Traffic and Logistics (T'L) in addition to _____.
   a. Free port
   b. Supply chain
   c. Consignor
   d. Purchasing

Chapter 8. Inventory

12. A _____ has several related meanings:

- a daily record of events or business; a private _____ is usually referred to as a diary.
- a newspaper or other periodical, in the literal sense of one published each day;
- many publications issued at stated intervals, such as magazines, or scholarly academic _____s, or the record of the transactions of a society, are often called _____s. Although _____ is sometimes used, erroneously, as a synonym for 'magazine,' in academic use, a _____ refers to a serious, scholarly publication, most often peer-reviewed. A non-scholarly magazine written for an educated audience about an industry or an area of professional activity is usually called a professional magazine.

The word 'journalist' for one whose business is writing for the public press has been in use since the end of the 17th century.

Open access _____s are scholarly _____s that are available to the reader without financial or other barrier other than access to the internet itself. Some are subsidized, and some require payment on behalf of the author. Subsidized _____s are financed by an academic institution or a government information center.

a. Journal
b. BNSF Railway
c. BMC Software, Inc.
d. 3M Company

13. Discounting is a financial mechanism in which a debtor obtains the right to delay payments to a creditor, for a defined period of time, in exchange for a charge or fee. Essentially, the party that owes money in the present purchases the right to delay the payment until some future date. The _____, or charge, is simply the difference between the original amount owed in the present and the amount that has to be paid in the future to settle the debt.
a. Discount factor
b. Discount
c. Discounting
d. Risk aversion

14. Transport or _____ is the movement of people and goods from one location to another. Transport is performed by various modes, such as air, rail, road, water, cable, pipeline and space. The field can be divided into infrastructure, vehicles, and operations.
a. Transportation
b. BNSF Railway
c. BMC Software, Inc.
d. 3M Company

15. In finance, a _____ is a debt security, in which the authorized issuer owes the holders a debt and, depending on the terms of the _____, is obliged to pay interest (the coupon) and/or to repay the principal at a later date, termed maturity. It is a formal contract to repay borrowed money with interest at fixed intervals.

Thus a _____ is like a loan: the issuer is the borrower, the _____ holder is the lender, and the coupon is the interest.

   a. Coupon rate
   b. Revenue bonds
   c. Bond
   d. Zero-coupon bond

16. _____ are journal entries made at the end of an accounting period to transfer temporary accounts to permanent accounts. An 'income summary' account may be used to show the balance between revenue and expenses, or they could be directly closed against retained earnings where dividend payments will be deducted from. This process is used to reset the balance of these temporary accounts to zero for the next accounting period.
   a. Closing entries
   b. Trial balance
   c. Treasury stock
   d. FIFO and LIFO accounting

17. In financial accounting the term inventory _____ is the loss of products between point of manufacture or purchase from supplier and point of sale. The term relates to the difference in the amount of margin or profit a retailer can obtain. If the amount of _____ is large, then profits go down which results in increased costs to the consumer to meet the needs of the retailer.
   a. Shrinkage
   b. Screening
   c. Maturity
   d. Homogeneous

18. _____ of something is, in finance, the adding together of interest or different investments over a period of time such as atoms (1 - the act or process of accruing; 2 - the amount that accrues.) It holds specific meanings in accounting and payroll.

_____, in accounting, describes the accounting method known as _____ basis, whereby revenues and expenses are recognized when they are accrued, i.e. accumulated (earned or incurred), regardless when the actual cash is received or paid out.

a. Accounts receivable
b. Assets
c. Accrual
d. Earnings before interest, taxes, depreciation and amortization

19. Under the average-cost method, it is assumed that the cost of inventory is based on the _____ of the goods available for sale during the period. _____ is computed by dividing the total cost of goods available for sale by the total units available for sale. This gives a weighted-average unit cost that is applied to the units in the ending inventory.
a. ABC Television Network
b. AIG
c. Ending inventory
d. Average cost

20. _____ is an acronym for First In, First Out, an abstraction in ways of organizing and manipulation of data relative to time and prioritization. This expression describes the principle of a queue processing technique or servicing conflicting demands by ordering process by first-come, first-served (FCFS) behaviour: what comes in first is handled first, what comes in next waits until the first is finished, etc.

Thus it is analogous to the behaviour of persons queueing (or 'standing in line', in common American parlance), where the persons leave the queue in the order they arrive, or waiting one's turn at a traffic control signal.

a. Kanban
b. FIFO
c. Trademark
d. Risk management

21. _____ methods are means of managing inventory and financial matters involving the money a company ties up within inventory of produced goods, raw materials, parts, components, or feed stocks. FIFO stands for first-in, first-out, meaning that the oldest inventory items are recorded as sold first. LIFO stands for last-in, first-out, meaning that the most recently purchased items are recorded as sold first.
a. FIFO and LIFO accounting
b. Finished good
c. Reorder point
d. 3M Company

Chapter 8. Inventory

22. _____ is one of a series of accounting transactions dealing with the billing of customers who owe money to a person, company or organization for goods and services that have been provided to the customer. In most business entities this is typically done by generating an invoice and mailing or electronically delivering it to the customer, who in turn must pay it within an established timeframe called credit or payment terms.

An example of a common payment term is Net 30, meaning payment is due in the amount of the invoice 30 days from the date of invoice.

  a. Accrued revenue
  b. Adjusting entries
  c. Accounts receivable
  d. Accrual

23. The _____ is an equation that equals the cost of goods sold divided by the average inventory. Average inventory equals beginning inventory plus ending inventory divided by 2.

The formula for _____:

$$\text{Inventory Turnover} = \frac{\text{Cost of Goods Sold}}{\text{Average Inventory}}$$

The formula for average inventory:

$$\text{Average Inventory} = \frac{\text{Beginning inventory} + \text{Ending inventory}}{2}$$

A low turnover rate may point to overstocking, obsolescence, or deficiencies in the product line or marketing effort.

  a. Inventory Turnover
  b. Upside potential ratio
  c. Enterprise Value/Sales
  d. Earnings per share

24. _____ is a file or account that contains money that a person or company owes to suppliers, but has not paid yet (a form of debt.) When you receive an invoice you add it to the file, and then you remove it when you pay. Thus, the A/P is a form of credit that suppliers offer to their purchasers by allowing them to pay for a product or service after it has already been received.

a. Accrual
b. Accounts payable
c. Earnings before interest, taxes, depreciation and amortization
d. Accounts receivable

25. _____ is an approach to valuing and reporting inventory. Normally ending inventory is stated at historical cost (what was paid to obtain it) but there are times when the original cost of the ending inventory is greater than the cost of replacement thus the inventory has lost value. If the inventory has decreased in value below historical cost then its carrying value is reduced and reported on the balance sheet.
   a. Bankruptcy prediction
   b. Lower of cost or market
   c. Remittance advice
   d. Certified Practising Accountant

26. _____ is a method of evaluating an asset's worth when held in inventory, in the field of accounting. _____ is part of the Generally Accepted Accounting Principles that apply to valuing inventory, so as to not overstate or understate the value of inventory goods. Net realisable value is generally equal to the selling price of the inventory goods less the selling costs (completion and disposal).
   a. BMC Software, Inc.
   b. Net realizable value
   c. Revenue recognition
   d. 3M Company

27. A _____ is any one of a variety of different systems, institutions, procedures, social relations and infrastructures whereby persons trade, and goods and services are exchanged, forming part of the economy. It is an arrangement that allows buyers and sellers to exchange things. _____s vary in size, range, geographic scale, location, types and variety of human communities, as well as the types of goods and services traded.
   a. Market Failure
   b. Perfect competition
   c. Recession
   d. Market

28. _____, Gross profit margin or Gross Profit Rate can be defined as the amount of contribution to the business enterprise, after paying for direct-fixed and direct-variable unit costs, required to cover overheads (fixed commitments) and provide a buffer for unknown items. It expresses the relationship between gross profit and sales revenue.

It can be expressed in absolute terms:

Gross Profit = Revenue − Cost of Goods Sold

or as the ratio of gross profit to sales revenue, usually in the form of a percentage:

_____ Percentage = (Revenue-Cost of Goods Sold)/Revenue

Cost of goods sold includes variable costs and fixed costs directly linked to the product, such as material and labor.

- a. BNSF Railway
- b. BMC Software, Inc.
- c. 3M Company
- d. Gross margin

29. _____ is the calculated approximation of a result which is usable even if input data may be incomplete or uncertain.

In statistics, see _____ theory, estimator.

In mathematics, approximation or _____ typically means finding upper or lower bounds of a quantity that cannot readily be computed precisely and is also an educated guess .

- a. AIG
- b. ABC Television Network
- c. AMEX
- d. Estimation

Chapter 9. Completing the Operating Cycle

1. Employment is a contract between two parties, one being the employer and the other being the _____. An _____ may be defined as: 'A person in the service of another under any contract of hire, express or implied, oral or written, where the employer has the power or right to control and direct the _____ in the material details of how the work is to be performed.' Black's Law Dictionary page 471 (5th ed. 1979.)
    a. ABC Television Network
    b. AMEX
    c. Employee
    d. AIG

2. A _____ is a compensation, usually financial, received by a worker in exchange for their labor.

Compensation in terms of _____s is given to worker and compensation in terms of salary is given to employees. Compensation is a monetary benefits given to employees in returns of the services provided by them.

    a. Wage
    b. BMC Software, Inc.
    c. 3M Company
    d. Retirement plan

3. In a company, _____ is the sum of all financial records of salaries, wages, bonuses and deductions.

A paycheck, is traditionally a paper document issued by an employer to pay an employee for services rendered. While most commonly used in the United States, recently the physical paycheck has been increasingly replaced by electronic direct deposit to bank accounts.

    a. Total Expense Ratio
    b. Tax expense
    c. Payroll
    d. 3M Company

4. A _____ is a fungible, negotiable instrument representing financial value. they are broadly categorized into debt securities (such as banknotes, bonds and debentures), and equity securities; e.g., common stocks. The company or other entity issuing the _____ is called the issuer.
    a. BMC Software, Inc.
    b. 3M Company
    c. Tracking stock
    d. Security

Chapter 9. Completing the Operating Cycle 79

5. _____ in the United States currently refers to the federal Old-Age, Survivors, and Disability Insurance (OASDI) program.

The original _____ Act and the current version of the Act, as amended encompass several social welfare and social insurance programs. The larger and better known programs are:

- Federal Old-Age, Survivors, and Disability Insurance
- Unemployment benefits
- Temporary Assistance for Needy Families
- Health Insurance for Aged and Disabled (Medicare)
- Grants to States for Medical Assistance Programs (Medicaid)
- State Children's Health Insurance Program (SCHIP)
- Supplemental Security Income (Social SecurityI)

U.S. _____ is a social insurance program funded through dedicated payroll taxes called Federal Insurance Contributions Act (FICA.) Tax deposits are formally entrusted to Federal Old-Age and Survivors Insurance Trust Fund, or Federal Disability Insurance Trust Fund, Federal Hospital Insurance Trust Fund or the Federal Supplementary Medical Insurance Trust Fund.

a. Comparable
b. Price-to-sales ratio
c. Social Security
d. Sale

6. _____, also called fair price (in a commonplace conflation of the two distinct concepts), is a concept used in finance and economics, defined as a rational and unbiased estimate of the potential market price of a good, service, or asset, taking into account such objective factors as:

- acquisition/production/distribution costs, replacement costs, or costs of close substitutes
- actual utility at a given level of development of social productive capability
- supply vs. demand

and subjective factors such as

- risk characteristics
- cost of capital
- individually perceived utility

In accounting, _____ is used as an estimate of the market value of an asset (or liability) for which a market price cannot be determined (usually because there is no established market for the asset.) Under GAAP (FAS 157), _____ is the amount at which the asset could be bought or sold in a current transaction between willing parties, or transferred to an equivalent party, other than in a liquidation sale. This is used for assets whose carrying value is based on mark-to-market valuations; for assets carried at historical cost, the _____ of the asset is not used. One example of where _____ is an issue is a College kitchen with a cost of $2 million which was built 5 years ago.

   a. BNSF Railway
   b. BMC Software, Inc.
   c. Fair value
   d. 3M Company

7. In finance, an _____ is a contract between a buyer and a seller that gives the buyer the right--but not the obligation-- to buy or to sell a particular asset (the underlying asset) at a later time at an agreed price. In return for granting the _____, the seller collects a payment (the premium) from the buyer. A call _____ gives the buyer the right to buy the underlying asset; a put _____ gives the buyer of the _____ the right to sell the underlying asset.

   a. AIG
   b. ABC Television Network
   c. Option
   d. AMEX

8. The term _____ or superannuation refers to a pension granted upon retirement. They may be set up by employers, insurance companies, the government or other institutions such as employer associations or trade unions.

   a. 3M Company
   b. BMC Software, Inc.
   c. Wage
   d. Retirement plan

9. In economics, a _____ is a type of pension plan in which an employer promises a specified monthly benefit on retirement that is predetermined by a formula based on the employee's earnings history, tenure of service and age, rather than depending on investment returns. It is 'defined' in the sense that the formula for computing the employer's contribution is known in advance. In the United States, 26 U.S.C.

   a. 3M Company
   b. BMC Software, Inc.
   c. Defined benefit pension plan
   d. Fixed asset turnover

Chapter 9. Completing the Operating Cycle

10. The Exxon Mobil Corporation is an American oil and gas corporation. It is a direct descendant of John D. Rockefeller's Standard Oil company, formed on November 30, 1999, by the merger of Exxon and Mobil.

_____ is the world's largest publicly traded company when measured by either revenue or market capitalization.

   a. Alan Greenspan
   b. Abby Joseph Cohen
   c. Arthur Betz Laffer
   d. ExxonMobil

11. _____ are formal records of a business' financial activities.

In British English, including United Kingdom company law, _____ are often referred to as accounts, although the term _____ is also used, particularly by accountants.

_____ provide an overview of a business' financial condition in both short and long term.

   a. 3M Company
   b. Financial statements
   c. Statement of retained earnings
   d. Notes to the financial statements

12. _____ is any physical or virtual entity that is owned by an individual or jointly by a group of individuals. An owner of _____ has the right to consume, sell, rent, mortgage, transfer and exchange his or her _____. Important widely-recognized types of _____ include real _____, personal _____ (other physical possessions), and intellectual _____ (rights over artistic creations, inventions, etc.), although the latter is not always as widely recognized or enforced.
   a. Fiduciary
   b. Primary authority
   c. Property
   d. Disclosure requirement

13. A _____ is the pinnacle activity involved in selling products or services in return for money or other compensation. It is an act of completion of a commercial activity.

A _____ is completed by the seller, the owner of the goods.

a. Tertiary sector of economy
b. Maturity
c. High yield stock
d. Sale

14. _____ of something is, in finance, the adding together of interest or different investments over a period of time such as atoms (1 - the act or process of accruing; 2 - the amount that accrues.) It holds specific meanings in accounting and payroll.

_____, in accounting, describes the accounting method known as _____ basis, whereby revenues and expenses are recognized when they are accrued, i.e. accumulated (earned or incurred), regardless when the actual cash is received or paid out.

a. Earnings before interest, taxes, depreciation and amortization
b. Accounts receivable
c. Assets
d. Accrual

15. An _____ is a tax levied on the financial income of people, corporations, or other legal entities. Various _____ systems exist, with varying degrees of tax incidence. Income taxation can be progressive, proportional, or regressive.

a. Individual Retirement Arrangement
b. Implied level of government service
c. Income Tax
d. Ordinary income

16. _____, in accrual accounting, is any account where the asset or liability is not realized until a future date (accounting period), e.g. annuities, charges, taxes, income, etc. The _____ item may be carried, dependent on type of deferral, as either an asset or liability.

a. Cash basis accounting
b. Payroll
c. Pro forma
d. Deferred

17. _____ is an accounting concept, meaning a future tax liability or asset, resulting from temporary differences between book (accounting) value of assets and liabilities and their tax value, or timing differences between the recognition of gains and losses in financial statements and their recognition in a tax computation.

Chapter 9. Completing the Operating Cycle

Temporary differences are differences between the carrying amount of an asset or liability recognised in the balance sheet and the amount attributed to that asset or liability for tax purposes (the tax base.)

a. Deficit
b. Tax refund
c. Deferred tax
d. Federal tax revenue by state

18. _____ that may or may not be incurred by an entity depending on the outcome of a future event such as a court case. These liabilities are recorded in a company's accounts and shown in the balance sheet when both probable and reasonably estimable. A footnote to the balance sheet describes the nature and extent of the _____.
    a. Nonacquiescence
    b. Tangible
    c. Headnote
    d. Contingent liabilities

19. In financial accounting, a _____ is defined as an obligation of an entity arising from past transactions or events, the settlement of which may result in the transfer or use of assets, provision of services or other yielding of economic benefits in the future.
    a. Vested
    b. Corporate governance
    c. Liability
    d. False Claims Act

Chapter 9. Completing the Operating Cycle

20. _____ means the giving out of information, either voluntarily or to be in compliance with legal regulations or workplace rules.

- In Computer security, full _____ means disclosing full information about vulnerabilities.
- In computing, _____ widget
- Journalism, full _____ refers to disclosing the interests of the writer which may bear on the subject being written about, for example, if the writer has worked with an interview subject in the past.

- In law:
  - The law of England and Wales, _____ refers to a process that may form part of legal proceedings, whereby parties inform to other parties the existence of any relevant documents that are, or have been, in their control. This compares with the process known as discovery in the course of legal proceedings in the United States.
  - In U.S. civil procedure (litigation rules for civil cases), _____ is a stage prior to trial. In civil cases, each party must disclose to the opposing party the following: names of witnesses which it may use to support its side, copies of documents (or mere description of these documents) in its control which it may use to support its side, computation of damages claimed, and certain insurance information. _____ is related to, but technically prior to, the discovery stage.
  - In Company law (known as 'corporate law' in the United States), _____ refers to giving out information about public or limited companies or their officers, which might be kept secret if the company was a private company or a partnership.

- In real property transactions, _____ refers to providing to a buyer information known to the seller or broker/agent concerning the condition or other aspects of real property that would affect the property's value or desirability. These rules regarding what information must be disclosed, and whether the information must be disclosed even if a buyer does not ask, vary from one jurisdiction to the next.

a. Controlled Foreign Corporations
b. Disclosure
c. Trailing
d. Tax harmonisation

21. In financial accounting and finance, _____ is the portion of receivables that can no longer be collected, typically from accounts receivable or loans. _____ in accounting is considered an expense.

There are two methods to account for _____:

1. Direct write off method (Non - GAAP)

A receivable which is not considered collectible is charged directly to the income statement.

1. Allowance method (GAAP)

Chapter 9. Completing the Operating Cycle 85

An estimate is made at the end of each fiscal year of the amount of _____. This is then accumulated in a provision which is then used to reduce specific receivable accounts as and when necessary.

a. Total Expense Ratio
b. 3M Company
c. Tax expense
d. Bad debt

22. _____ is that which is owed; usually referencing assets owed, but the term can also cover moral obligations and other interactions not requiring money. In the case of assets, _____ is a means of using future purchasing power in the present before a summation has been earned. Some companies and corporations use _____ as a part of their overall corporate finance strategy.
   a. Lender
   b. Loan
   c. Debenture
   d. Debt

23. In accounting, _____ has a very specific meaning. It is an outflow of cash or other valuable assets from a person or company to another person or company. This outflow of cash is generally one side of a trade for products or services that have equal or better current or future value to the buyer than to the seller.
   a. AIG
   b. AMEX
   c. ABC Television Network
   d. Expense

24. The phrase _____, according to the Organization for Economic Co-operation and Development, refers to 'creative work undertaken on a systematic basis in order to increase the stock of knowledge, including knowledge of man, culture and society, and the use of this stock of knowledge to devise new applications [sic]'

New product design and development is more than often a crucial factor in the survival of a company. In an industry that is fast changing, firms must continually revise their design and range of products. This is necessary due to continuous technology change and development as well as other competitors and the changing preference of customers.

Chapter 9. Completing the Operating Cycle

a. Research and development
b. BMC Software, Inc.
c. 3M Company
d. BNSF Railway

25. _____ is a company's financial statement that indicates how the revenue is transformed into the net income The purpose of the _____ is to show managers and investors whether the company made or lost money during the period being reported.

The important thing to remember about an _____ is that it represents a period of time.

a. Income statement
b. AMEX
c. ABC Television Network
d. AIG

26. _____ is revenue from peripheral (non-core) operations. For example, a company that manufactures and sells automobiles would record the revenue from the sale of an automobile as 'regular' revenue. If that same company also rented a portion of one of its buildings, it would record that revenue as e;_____e; and disclose it separately on its income statement to show that it is from something other than its core operations.

a. AIG
b. AMEX
c. ABC Television Network
d. Other revenue

27. _____ is a specific term used in companies' financial reporting from the company-whole point of view. Because that use excludes the effects of changing ownership interest, an economic measure of _____ is necessary for financial analysis from the shareholders' point of view

_____ is defined by the Financial Accounting Standards Board, or FASB, as 'the change in equity [net assets] of a business enterprise during a period from transactions and other events and circumstances from nonowner sources. It includes all changes in equity during a period except those resulting from investments by owners and distributions to owners.'

_____ is the sum of net income and other items that must bypass the income statement because they have not been realized, including items like an unrealized holding gain or loss from available for sale securities and foreign currency translation gains or losses.

a. Comprehensive income
b. BNSF Railway
c. 3M Company
d. BMC Software, Inc.

28. _____ are the earnings returned on the initial investment amount.

In the US, the Financial Accounting Standards Board (FASB) requires companies' income statements to report _____ for each of the major categories of the income statement: continuing operations, discontinued operations, extraordinary items, and net income.

The _____ formula does not include preferred dividends for categories outside of continued operations and net income.

a. Earnings per share
b. Earnings yield
c. Average accounting return
d. Invested capital

29. _____ is a company's earnings per share (EPS) calculated using fully diluted shares outstanding. _____ indicates a 'worst case' scenario, one in which everyone who could have received stock without purchasing it directly for the full market value did so.

To find _____, basic EPS is calculated for each of the categories on the income statement first. Then each of the dilutive securities are ranked based on their effects, from most dilutive to least dilutive and antidilutive. Then the basic EPS number is diluted one by one by applying each one, skipping any instruments that have an antidilutive effect.

a. Financial ratio
b. Return on assets Du Pont
c. Cash conversion cycle
d. Diluted earnings per share

Chapter 10. Investments in Property, Plant, and Equipment and in Intangible Assets

1. In business and accounting, _____ are everything of value that is owned by a person or company. It is a claim on the property your income of a borrower. The balance sheet of a firm records the monetary value of the _____ owned by the firm.
   a. Assets
   b. Accrual basis accounting
   c. Earnings before interest, taxes, depreciation and amortization
   d. Accounts receivable

2. _____ are defined as identifiable non-monetary assets that cannot be seen, touched or physically measured, which are created through time and/or effort and that are identifiable as a separate asset. There are two primary forms of intangibles - legal intangibles (such as trade secrets (e.g., customer lists), copyrights, patents, trademarks, and goodwill) and competitive intangibles (such as knowledge activities (know-how, knowledge), collaboration activities, leverage activities, and structural activities.) Legal intangibles are known under the generic term intellectual property and generate legal property rights defensible in a court of law.
   a. AIG
   b. ABC Television Network
   c. Overhead
   d. Intangible assets

3. In economic models, the _____ time frame assumes no fixed factors of production. Firms can enter or leave the marketplace, and the cost (and availability) of land, labor, raw materials, and capital goods can be assumed to vary. In contrast, in the short-run time frame, certain factors are assumed to be fixed, because there is not sufficient time for them to change.
   a. 3M Company
   b. BMC Software, Inc.
   c. Short-run
   d. Long-run

4. _____ is any physical or virtual entity that is owned by an individual or jointly by a group of individuals. An owner of _____ has the right to consume, sell, rent, mortgage, transfer and exchange his or her _____. Important widely-recognized types of _____ include real _____, personal _____ (other physical possessions), and intellectual _____ (rights over artistic creations, inventions, etc.), although the latter is not always as widely recognized or enforced.
   a. Property
   b. Fiduciary
   c. Primary authority
   d. Disclosure requirement

Chapter 10. Investments in Property, Plant, and Equipment and in Intangible Assets

5. _____, also known as property, plant, and equipment (PP&E), is a term used in accountancy for assets and property which cannot easily be converted into cash. This can be compared with current assets such as cash or bank accounts, which are described as liquid assets. In most cases, only tangible assets are referred to as fixed.
   a. Minority interest
   b. Subledger
   c. Bankruptcy prediction
   d. Fixed asset

6. An _____ is the buying of one company by another. An _____ may be friendly or hostile. In the former case, the companies cooperate in negotiations; in the latter case, the takeover target is unwilling to be bought or the target's board has no prior knowledge of the offer. _____ usually refers to a purchase of a smaller firm by a larger one. Sometimes, however, a smaller firm will acquire management control of a larger or longer established company and keep its name for the combined entity. This is known as a reverse takeover.
   a. Acquisition
   b. AMEX
   c. ABC Television Network
   d. AIG

7. _____ is a process by which a firm can obtain the use of a certain fixed assets for which it must pay a series of contractual, periodic, tax deductable payments. The lessee is the receiver of the services or the assets under the lease contract and the lessor is the owner of the assets. The relationship between the tenant and the landlord is called a tenancy, and can be for a fixed or an indefinite period of time (called the term of the lease.)
   a. Leasing
   b. Federal Sentencing Guidelines
   c. Resource Conservation and Recovery Act
   d. Property

8. In economics, _____ or _____ goods or real _____ refers to factors of production used to create goods or services that are not themselves significantly consumed (though they may depreciate) in the production process. _____ goods may be acquired with money or financial _____. In finance and accounting, _____ generally refers to financial wealth, especially that used to start or maintain a business.
   a. Vyborg Appeal
   b. Screening
   c. Disclosure
   d. Capital

Chapter 10. Investments in Property, Plant, and Equipment and in Intangible Assets

9. _____ is the planning process used to determine whether a firm's long term investments such as new machinery, replacement machinery, new plants, new products, and research development projects are worth pursuing. It is budget for major capital, or investment, expenditures.

Many formal methods are used in _____, including the techniques such as

- Net present value
- Profitability index
- Internal rate of return
- Modified Internal Rate of Return
- Equivalent annuity

These methods use the incremental cash flows from each potential investment, or project. Techniques based on accounting earnings and accounting rules are sometimes used - though economists consider this to be improper - such as the accounting rate of return, and 'return on investment.' Simplified and hybrid methods are used as well, such as payback period and discounted payback period.

a. Preferred stock
b. Gross profit
c. Cash flow
d. Capital budgeting

10. Simply put, _____ is the value of money figuring in a given amount of interest for a given amount of time. For example 100 dollars of todays money held for a year at 5 percent interest is worth 105 dollars, therefore 100 dollars paid now or 105 dollars paid exactly one year from now is the same amount of payment of money with that given intersest at that given amount of time. This notion dates at least to Martín de Azpilcueta of the School of Salamanca.

a. Merck ' Co., Inc.
b. Collusion
c. Competition law
d. Time value of money

11. A _____ is a fungible, negotiable instrument representing financial value. they are broadly categorized into debt securities (such as banknotes, bonds and debentures), and equity securities; e.g., common stocks. The company or other entity issuing the _____ is called the issuer.

a. Security
b. BMC Software, Inc.
c. Tracking stock
d. 3M Company

Chapter 10. Investments in Property, Plant, and Equipment and in Intangible Assets

12. In economics, business, retail, and accounting, a _____ is the value of money that has been used up to produce something, and hence is not available for use anymore. In economics, a _____ is an alternative that is given up as a result of a decision. In business, the _____ may be one of acquisition, in which case the amount of money expended to acquire it is counted as _____.
   a. Cost of quality
   b. Cost allocation
   c. Prime cost
   d. Cost

13. An _____ is a lease whose term is short compared to the useful life of the asset or piece of equipment (an airliner, a ship etc.) being leased. An _____ is commonly used to acquire equipment on a relatively short-term basis.
   a. Express warranty
   b. Employee Retirement Income Security Act
   c. Operating lease
   d. Issued shares

14. A _____ is a contract conferring a right on one person to possess property belonging to another person (called a landlord or lessor) to the exclusion of the owner landlord. It is a rental agreement between landlord and tenant. The relationship between the tenant and the landlord is called a tenancy, and the right to possession by the tenant is sometimes called a leasehold interest.
   a. Robinson-Patman Act
   b. Federal Sentencing Guidelines
   c. Model Code of Professional Responsibility
   d. Lease

15. _____ is a fee paid on borrowed assets. It is the price paid for the use of borrowed money, or, money earned by deposited funds. Assets that are sometimes lent with _____ include money, shares, consumer goods through hire purchase, major assets such as aircraft, and even entire factories in finance lease arrangements. The _____ is calculated upon the value of the assets in the same manner as upon money.
   a. ABC Television Network
   b. AIG
   c. Interest
   d. Insolvency

16. _____ is a term used in accounting, economics and finance to spread the cost of an asset over the span of several years.

In simple words we can say that _____ is the reduction in the value of an asset due to usage, passage of time, wear and tear, technological outdating or obsolescence, depletion, inadequacy, rot, rust, decay or other such factors.

In accounting, _____ is a term used to describe any method of attributing the historical or purchase cost of an asset across its useful life, roughly corresponding to normal wear and tear.

   a. Current asset
   b. Net profit
   c. General ledger
   d. Depreciation

17.   In financial accounting and finance, _____ is the portion of receivables that can no longer be collected, typically from accounts receivable or loans. _____ in accounting is considered an expense.

There are two methods to account for _____:

   1.   Direct write off method (Non - GAAP)

A receivable which is not considered collectible is charged directly to the income statement.

   1.   Allowance method (GAAP)

An estimate is made at the end of each fiscal year of the amount of _____. This is then accumulated in a provision which is then used to reduce specific receivable accounts as and when necessary.

   a. 3M Company
   b. Total Expense Ratio
   c. Bad debt
   d. Tax expense

18.   _____ is that which is owed; usually referencing assets owed, but the term can also cover moral obligations and other interactions not requiring money. In the case of assets, _____ is a means of using future purchasing power in the present before a summation has been earned. Some companies and corporations use _____ as a part of their overall corporate finance strategy.

Chapter 10. Investments in Property, Plant, and Equipment and in Intangible Assets

a. Debt
b. Debenture
c. Loan
d. Lender

19. In accounting, _____ has a very specific meaning. It is an outflow of cash or other valuable assets from a person or company to another person or company. This outflow of cash is generally one side of a trade for products or services that have equal or better current or future value to the buyer than to the seller.
    a. AMEX
    b. AIG
    c. ABC Television Network
    d. Expense

20. In accounting, _____ or carrying value is the value of an asset according to its balance sheet account balance. For assets, the value is based on the original cost of the asset less any depreciation, amortization or impairment costs made against the asset. Traditionally, a company's _____ is its total assets minus intangible assets and liabilities.
    a. Matching principle
    b. Generally accepted accounting principles
    c. Depreciation
    d. Book value

21. Straight-line depreciation is the simplest and most often used technique, in which the company estimates the _____ of the asset at the end of the period during which it will be used to generate revenues (useful life), and will expense a portion of original cost in equal increments over that period. The _____ is an estimate of the value of the asset at the time it will be sold or disposed of; it may be zero. _____ is scrap value, by another name.
    a. Closing entries
    b. Generally accepted accounting principles
    c. Net profit
    d. Salvage value

22. There are several methods for calculating depreciation, generally based on either the passage of time or the level of activity (or use) of the asset.

_____ is the simplest and most often used technique, in which the company estimates the salvage value of the asset at the end of the period during which it will be used to generate revenues (useful life), and will expense a portion of original cost in equal increments over that period.

a. Straight-line depreciation
b. Current asset
c. Pro forma
d. Closing entries

23. In finance, a _____ is a debt security, in which the authorized issuer owes the holders a debt and, depending on the terms of the _____, is obliged to pay interest (the coupon) and/or to repay the principal at a later date, termed maturity. It is a formal contract to repay borrowed money with interest at fixed intervals.

Thus a _____ is like a loan: the issuer is the borrower, the _____ holder is the lender, and the coupon is the interest.

a. Coupon rate
b. Bond
c. Revenue bonds
d. Zero-coupon bond

24. A _____ is any one of a variety of different systems, institutions, procedures, social relations and infrastructures whereby persons trade, and goods and services are exchanged, forming part of the economy. It is an arrangement that allows buyers and sellers to exchange things. _____s vary in size, range, geographic scale, location, types and variety of human communities, as well as the types of goods and services traded.
a. Market Failure
b. Perfect competition
c. Recession
d. Market

25. _____ is the price at which an asset would trade in a competitive Walrasian auction setting. _____ is often used interchangeably with open _____, fair value or fair _____, although these terms have distinct definitions in different standards, and may differ in some circumstances.

International Valuation Standards defines _____ as 'the estimated amount for which a property should exchange on the date of valuation between a willing buyer and a willing seller in an arme;s-length transaction after proper marketing wherein the parties had each acted knowledgeably, prudently, and without compulsion.'

_____ is a concept distinct from market price, which is e;the price at which one can transacte;, while _____ is e;the true underlying valuee; according to theoretical standards.

Chapter 10. Investments in Property, Plant, and Equipment and in Intangible Assets 95

a. Sinking fund
b. Debtor
c. Segregated portfolio company
d. Market value

26. In physics, and more specifically kinematics, _____ is the change in velocity over time. Because velocity is a vector, it can change in two ways: a change in magnitude and/or a change in direction. In one dimension, _____ is the rate at which something speeds up or slows down.

a. AMEX
b. AIG
c. ABC Television Network
d. Acceleration

27. A _____ is a set of exclusive rights granted by a state to an inventor or his assignee for a limited period of time in exchange for a disclosure of an invention.

The procedure for granting _____s, the requirements placed on the _____ee and the extent of the exclusive rights vary widely between countries according to national laws and international agreements. Typically, however, a _____ application must include one or more claims defining the invention which must be new, inventive, and useful or industrially applicable.

a. Patent
b. Negligence
c. Trust indenture
d. FLSA

28. A _____ or trade mark, identified by the symbols ™ (not yet registered) and ® (registered), is a distinctive sign or indicator used by an individual, business organization or other legal entity to identify that the products and/or services to consumers with which the _____ appears originate from a unique source, and to distinguish its products or services from those of other entities. A _____ is a type of intellectual property, and typically a name, word, phrase, logo, symbol, design, image, or a combination of these elements. There is also a range of non-conventional _____s comprising marks which do not fall into these standard categories.

a. FIFO
b. Risk management
c. Kanban
d. Trademark

Chapter 10. Investments in Property, Plant, and Equipment and in Intangible Assets

29. _____, also called fair price (in a commonplace conflation of the two distinct concepts), is a concept used in finance and economics, defined as a rational and unbiased estimate of the potential market price of a good, service, or asset, taking into account such objective factors as:

- acquisition/production/distribution costs, replacement costs, or costs of close substitutes
- actual utility at a given level of development of social productive capability
- supply vs. demand

and subjective factors such as

- risk characteristics
- cost of capital
- individually perceived utility

In accounting, _____ is used as an estimate of the market value of an asset (or liability) for which a market price cannot be determined (usually because there is no established market for the asset.) Under GAAP (FAS 157), _____ is the amount at which the asset could be bought or sold in a current transaction between willing parties, or transferred to an equivalent party, other than in a liquidation sale. This is used for assets whose carrying value is based on mark-to-market valuations; for assets carried at historical cost, the _____ of the asset is not used. One example of where _____ is an issue is a College kitchen with a cost of $2 million which was built 5 years ago.

   a. BNSF Railway
   b. BMC Software, Inc.
   c. 3M Company
   d. Fair value

30. _____ is the calculated approximation of a result which is usable even if input data may be incomplete or uncertain.

In statistics, see _____ theory, estimator.

In mathematics, approximation or _____ typically means finding upper or lower bounds of a quantity that cannot readily be computed precisely and is also an educated guess .

   a. AIG
   b. ABC Television Network
   c. AMEX
   d. Estimation

Chapter 10. Investments in Property, Plant, and Equipment and in Intangible Assets 97

31. _____ is the process of increasing, or accounting for, an amount over a period of time. Particular instances of the term include:

- _____, the allocation of a lump sum amount to different time periods, particularly for loans and other forms of finance, including related interest or other finance charges.
    - _____ schedule, a table detailing each periodic payment on a loan (typically a mortgage), as generated by an _____ calculator.
    - Negative _____, an _____ schedule where the loan amount actually increases through not paying the full interest
- Amortized analysis, analyzing the execution cost of algorithms over a sequence of operations.
- _____ of capital expenditures of certain assets under accounting rules, particularly intangible assets, in a manner analogous to depreciation.
- _____

a. Intangible
b. Annuity
c. EBIT
d. Amortization

32. _____ is the ratio of sales (on the Profit and loss account) to the value of fixed assets (on the balance sheet.) It indicates how well the business is using its fixed assets to generate sales.

$$Fixed\ Asset\ Turnover = \frac{Sales}{Average\ net\ fixed\ assets}$$

Generally speaking, the higher the ratio, the better, because a high ratio indicates the business has less money tied up in fixed assets for each dollar of sales revenue.

a. Fixed asset turnover
b. Defined benefit pension plan
c. BMC Software, Inc.
d. 3M Company

33. _____ is one of a series of accounting transactions dealing with the billing of customers who owe money to a person, company or organization for goods and services that have been provided to the customer. In most business entities this is typically done by generating an invoice and mailing or electronically delivering it to the customer, who in turn must pay it within an established timeframe called credit or payment terms.

An example of a common payment term is Net 30, meaning payment is due in the amount of the invoice 30 days from the date of invoice.

a. Accrual
b. Accrued revenue
c. Adjusting entries
d. Accounts receivable

34. _____ is a financial ratio that measures the efficiency of a company's use of its assets in generating sales revenue or sales income to the company.

$$Asset\ Turnover = \frac{Sales}{Average Total Assets}$$

- 'Sales' is the value of 'Net Sales' or 'Sales' from the company's income statement
- 'Average Total Assets' is the value of 'Total assets' from the company's balance sheet in the beginning and the end of the fiscal period divided by 2.

a. Information ratio
b. Enterprise Value/Sales
c. Average propensity to consume
d. Asset Turnover

35. _____ refers to any one of several methods by which a company, for 'financial accounting' and/or tax purposes, depreciates a fixed asset in such a way that the amount of depreciation taken each year is higher during the earlier years of an assete;s life. For financial accounting purposes, _____ is generally used when an asset is expected to be much more productive during its early years, so that depreciation expense will more accurately represent how much of an assete;s usefulness is being used up each year. For tax purposes, _____ provides a way of deferring corporate income taxes by reducing taxable income in current years, in exchange for increased taxable income in future years.

a. Accelerated depreciation
b. Effective marginal tax rates
c. Indirect tax
d. User charge

36. The _____ is the current method of accelerated asset depreciation required by the United States income tax code. Under _____, all assets are divided into classes which dictate the number of years over which an asset's cost will be recovered.

Prior to the Accelerated Cost Recovery System (ACRS), most capital purchases were depreciated using a straight line technique, that allowed for the depreciation of the asset over its useful life.

Chapter 10. Investments in Property, Plant, and Equipment and in Intangible Assets

a. BMC Software, Inc.
b. 3M Company
c. Modified Accelerated Cost Recovery System
d. Categorical grants

37. An _____ is a tax levied on the financial income of people, corporations, or other legal entities. Various _____ systems exist, with varying degrees of tax incidence. Income taxation can be progressive, proportional, or regressive.
a. Ordinary income
b. Implied level of government service
c. Individual Retirement Arrangement
d. Income tax

Chapter 11. Long-Term Debt Financing

1. _____ measures the nominal future sum of money that a given sum of money is 'worth' at a specified time in the future assuming a certain interest rate rate of return; it is the present value multiplied by the accumulation function.

The value does not include corrections for inflation or other factors that affect the true value of money in the future. This is used in time value of money calculations.

   a. 3M Company
   b. Future value
   c. Present value
   d. Net present value

2. In financial accounting, a _____ is defined as an obligation of an entity arising from past transactions or events, the settlement of which may result in the transfer or use of assets, provision of services or other yielding of economic benefits in the future.
   a. Liability
   b. Vested
   c. Corporate governance
   d. False Claims Act

3. In economic models, the _____ time frame assumes no fixed factors of production. Firms can enter or leave the marketplace, and the cost (and availability) of land, labor, raw materials, and capital goods can be assumed to vary. In contrast, in the short-run time frame, certain factors are assumed to be fixed, because there is not sufficient time for them to change.
   a. Long-run
   b. Short-run
   c. BMC Software, Inc.
   d. 3M Company

4. _____ are liabilities with a future benefit over one year, such as notes payable that mature greater than one year.

In accounting, the _____ are shown on the right wing of the balance-sheet representing the sources of funds, which are generally bounded in form of capital assets.

Examples of _____ are debentures, mortgage loans and other bank loans (note: not all bank loans are long term as not all are paid over a period greater than a year, the example is bridging loan.)

Chapter 11. Long-Term Debt Financing

a. Gross sales
b. Cash basis accounting
c. Book value
d. Long-term liabilities

5. _____ is the value on a given date of a future payment or series of future payments, discounted to reflect the time value of money and other factors such as investment risk. _____ calculations are widely used in business and economics to provide a means to compare cash flows at different times on a meaningful 'like to like' basis.

The most commonly applied model of the time value of money is compound interest.

a. Net present value
b. 3M Company
c. Future value
d. Present value

6. The term _____ is used in finance theory to refer to any terminating stream of fixed payments over a specified period of time. This usage is most commonly seen in academic discussions of finance, usually in connection with the valuation of the stream of payments, taking into account time value of money concepts such as interest rate and future value.

Examples of these are regular deposits to a savings account, monthly home mortgage payments and monthly insurance payments.

a. Improvement
b. Appropriation
c. Intangible
d. Annuity

7. In vector calculus, _____ is a vector differential operator represented by the nabla symbol: ∇.

_____ is a mathematical tool serving primarily as a convention for mathematical notation; it makes many equations easier to comprehend, write, and remember. Depending on the way _____ is applied, it can describe the gradient (slope), divergence (degree to which something converges or diverges) or curl (rotational motion at points in a fluid.)

Chapter 11. Long-Term Debt Financing

a. 3M Company
b. BMC Software, Inc.
c. BNSF Railway
d. Del

8. A _____ is the transfer of wealth from one party (such as a person or company) to another. A _____ is usually made in exchange for the provision of goods, services or both, or to fulfill a legal obligation.

The simplest and oldest form of _____ is barter, the exchange of one good or service for another.

a. Payee
b. Payment
c. 3M Company
d. BMC Software, Inc.

9. A _____ is a fungible, negotiable instrument representing financial value. they are broadly categorized into debt securities (such as banknotes, bonds and debentures), and equity securities; e.g., common stocks. The company or other entity issuing the _____ is called the issuer.
a. Tracking stock
b. 3M Company
c. BMC Software, Inc.
d. Security

10. _____ is a fee paid on borrowed assets. It is the price paid for the use of borrowed money , or, money earned by deposited funds .Assets that are sometimes lent with _____ include money, shares, consumer goods through hire purchase, major assets such as aircraft, and even entire factories in finance lease arrangements. The _____ is calculated upon the value of the assets in the same manner as upon money.
a. Interest
b. ABC Television Network
c. Insolvency
d. AIG

11. A _____ is the transfer of an interest in property (or the equivalent in law - a charge) to a lender as a security for a debt - usually a loan of money. While a _____ in itself is not a debt, it is the lender's security for a debt. It is a transfer of an interest in land (or the equivalent) from the owner to the _____ lender, on the condition that this interest will be returned to the owner when the terms of the _____ have been satisfied or performed.

Chapter 11. Long-Term Debt Financing

a. BNSF Railway
b. BMC Software, Inc.
c. 3M Company
d. Mortgage

12. An _____ is the price a borrower pays for the use of money they do not own, for instance a small company might borrow from a bank to kick start their business, and the return a lender receives for deferring the use of funds, by lending it to the borrower. _____s are normally expressed as a percentage rate over the period of one year.

_____s targets are also a vital tool of monetary policy and are used to control variables like investment, inflation, and unemployment.

a. ABC Television Network
b. Interest rate
c. AMEX
d. AIG

13. _____ is the process of increasing, or accounting for, an amount over a period of time. Particular instances of the term include:

- _____, the allocation of a lump sum amount to different time periods, particularly for loans and other forms of finance, including related interest or other finance charges.
    - _____ schedule, a table detailing each periodic payment on a loan (typically a mortgage), as generated by an _____ calculator.
    - Negative _____, an _____ schedule where the loan amount actually increases through not paying the full interest
- Amortized analysis, analyzing the execution cost of algorithms over a sequence of operations.
- _____ of capital expenditures of certain assets under accounting rules, particularly intangible assets, in a manner analogous to depreciation.
- _____

a. Intangible
b. Annuity
c. EBIT
d. Amortization

14. A _____ is a contract conferring a right on one person to possess property belonging to another person (called a landlord or lessor) to the exclusion of the owner landlord. It is a rental agreement between landlord and tenant. The relationship between the tenant and the landlord is called a tenancy, and the right to possession by the tenant is sometimes called a leasehold interest.

a. Lease
b. Model Code of Professional Responsibility
c. Federal Sentencing Guidelines
d. Robinson-Patman Act

15. An _____ is a lease whose term is short compared to the useful life of the asset or piece of equipment (an airliner, a ship etc.) being leased. An _____ is commonly used to acquire equipment on a relatively short-term basis.

a. Employee Retirement Income Security Act
b. Express warranty
c. Issued shares
d. Operating lease

16. In finance, a _____ is a debt security, in which the authorized issuer owes the holders a debt and, depending on the terms of the _____, is obliged to pay interest (the coupon) and/or to repay the principal at a later date, termed maturity. It is a formal contract to repay borrowed money with interest at fixed intervals.

Thus a _____ is like a loan: the issuer is the borrower, the _____ holder is the lender, and the coupon is the interest.

a. Revenue bonds
b. Zero-coupon bond
c. Coupon rate
d. Bond

17. A _____ is defined as a certificate of agreement of loans which is given under the company's stamp and carries an undertaking that the _____ holder will get a fixed return (fixed on the basis of interest rates) and the principal amount whenever the _____ matures.

In finance, a _____ is a long-term debt instrument used by governments and large companies to obtain funds. It is defined as 'any form of borrowing that commits a firm to pay interest and repay capital.

a. Credit rating
b. Loan
c. Debenture
d. Loan to value

18. A _____ is a type of bond that allows the issuer of the bond to retain the privilege of redeeming the bond at some point before the bond reaches the date of maturity. In other words, on the call dates, the issuer has the right, but not the obligation, to buy back the bonds from the bond holders at the call price. Technically speaking, the bonds are not really bought and held by the issuer but cancelled immediately.
   a. Zero-coupon
   b. Catastrophe bonds
   c. Coupon rate
   d. Callable bond

19. _____ is a legal document issued to lenders and describes key terms such as the interest rate, maturity date, convertibility, pledge, promises, representations, covenants, and other terms of the bond offering. When the Offering Memorandum is prepared in advance of marketing a Bond, the indenture will typically be summarised in the 'Description of Notes' section.
   a. Bond indenture
   b. Consumer protection laws
   c. Leasing
   d. Malpractice

20. In finance, a _____ is a type of bond that can be converted into shares of stock in the issuing company, usually at some pre-announced ratio. It is a hybrid security with debt- and equity-like features. Although it typically has a low coupon rate, the holder is compensated with the ability to convert the bond to common stock, usually at a substantial discount to the stock's market value.
   a. Zero-coupon bond
   b. Coupon rate
   c. Zero-coupon
   d. Convertible bond

21. In marketing a _____ is a ticket or document that can be exchanged for a financial discount or rebate when purchasing a product. Customarily, _____s are issued by manufacturers of consumer packaged goods or by retailers, to be used in retail stores as a part of sales promotions. They are often widely distributed through mail, magazines, newspapers, the Internet, and mobile devices such as cell phones.
   a. BMC Software, Inc.
   b. 3M Company
   c. Merchandising
   d. Coupon

Chapter 11. Long-Term Debt Financing

22. _____ is the value of a coin, stamp or paper money, as printed on the coin, stamp or bill itself by the minting authority. While the _____ usually refers to the true value of the coin, stamp or bill in question (as with circulation coins) it can sometimes be largely symbolic, as is often the case with bullion coins. For example, a one troy ounce (31 g) American Gold Eagle bullion coin was worth and sold for about $670 USD during 2006 market prices (as of July 17, 2006) and yet has a _____ of only $50 USD.

   a. Face value
   b. BNSF Railway
   c. 3M Company
   d. BMC Software, Inc.

23. In economics, a _____ is a lower rated, potentially higher paying bond.

   - High-yield debt

A high-risk, non-investment-grade bond with a low credit rating, usually BB or lower; as a consequence, it usually has a high yield. opposite of investment-grade bond. This content can be found on the following page:

.

   a. BMC Software, Inc.
   b. 3M Company
   c. BNSF Railway
   d. Junk bond

24. _____ is a life of security. It may also refer to the final payment date of a loan or other financial instrument, at which point all remaining interest and principal is due to be paid.

1, 3, 6 months _____ band can be calculated by using 30-day per month periods. For _____ bands over a year it is acceptable to use 365 day per year. For example with a Treasury Bond, its _____ is the date on which the principal is paid.

   a. Statements of Financial Accounting Standards No. 133, Accounting for Derivative
   Instruments and Hedging Activities
   b. Maturity
   c. The Goodyear Tire ' Rubber Company
   d. Factor

25. _____ are financial bonds that mature in installments over a period of time. In effect, a $100,000, 5-year serial bond would mature in a $20,000 annuity over a 5-year interval. Bond issues consisting of a series of blocks of securities maturing in sequence, the coupon rate can be different.

Chapter 11. Long-Term Debt Financing

a. Just-in-time
b. Low Income Housing Tax Credit
c. Household and Dependent Care Credit
d. Serial bonds

26. A _____ is a bond bought at a price lower than its face value, with the face value repaid at the time of maturity. It does not make periodic interest payments, or so-called 'coupons,' hence the term _____. Investors earn return from the compounded interest all paid at maturity plus the difference between the discounted price of the bond and its par value.
    a. Callable bond
    b. Municipal bond
    c. Premium bond
    d. Zero-coupon bond

27. Discounting is a financial mechanism in which a debtor obtains the right to delay payments to a creditor, for a defined period of time, in exchange for a charge or fee. Essentially, the party that owes money in the present purchases the right to delay the payment until some future date. The _____, or charge, is simply the difference between the original amount owed in the present and the amount that has to be paid in the future to settle the debt.
    a. Discount factor
    b. Risk aversion
    c. Discounting
    d. Discount

28. An _____ is a legal contract between two parties, particularly for indentured labour or a term of apprenticeship but also for certain land transactions. The term comes from the medieval English '_____ of retainer' -- a legal contract written in duplicate on the same sheet, with the copies separated by cutting along a jagged line so that the teeth of the two parts could later be refitted to confirm authenticity. Each party to the deed would then retain a part.
    a. Operating Lease
    b. Impracticability
    c. Employee Retirement Income Security Act
    d. Indenture

29. A _____ bond is a bond bought at a price lower than its face value, with the face value repaid at the time of maturity. It does not make periodic interest payments, or have so-called 'coupons,' hence the term _____ bond. Investors earn return from the compounded interest all paid at maturity plus the difference between the discounted price of the bond and its par value.

a. Callable bond
b. Zero-coupon
c. Catastrophe bonds
d. Municipal bond

30. _____ in economics and business is the result of an exchange and from that trade we assign a numerical monetary value to a good, service or asset. If Alice trades Bob 4 apples for an orange, the _____ of an orange is 4 apples. Inversely, the _____ of an apple is 1/4 oranges.
   a. Discounts and allowances
   b. Price
   c. Transactional Net Margin Method
   d. Price discrimination

31. A _____ is any one of a variety of different systems, institutions, procedures, social relations and infrastructures whereby persons trade, and goods and services are exchanged, forming part of the economy. It is an arrangement that allows buyers and sellers to exchange things. _____s vary in size, range, geographic scale, location, types and variety of human communities, as well as the types of goods and services traded.
   a. Perfect competition
   b. Recession
   c. Market
   d. Market Failure

32. In finance, the term _____ describes the amount in cash that returns to the owners of a security. Normally it does not include the price variations, at the difference of the total return. _____ applies to various stated rates of return on stocks (common and preferred, and convertible), fixed income instruments (bonds, notes, bills, strips, zero coupon), and some other investment type insurance products (e.g. annuities.)
   a. Pension System
   b. Residence trusts
   c. Disclosure
   d. Yield

33. A _____ is like a lottery bond issued by the United Kingdom government's National Savings and Investments scheme. The government promises to buy back the bond, on request, for its original price.

_____s were introduced by the government in 1956, with the aim of encouraging saving and controlling inflation, with the first bonds going on sale on 1 November of that year.

a. Revenue bonds
b. Zero-coupon bond
c. Callable bond
d. Premium Bond

34. _____ is that which is owed; usually referencing assets owed, but the term can also cover moral obligations and other interactions not requiring money. In the case of assets, _____ is a means of using future purchasing power in the present before a summation has been earned. Some companies and corporations use _____ as a part of their overall corporate finance strategy.
   a. Debenture
   b. Loan
   c. Debt
   d. Lender

35. _____ is a financial ratio that indicates the percentage of a company's assets are provided via debt. It is the ratio of total debt (the sum of current liabilities and long-term liabilities) and total assets (the sum of current assets, fixed assets, and other assets such as 'goodwill'.)

$$\text{Debt ratio} = \frac{\text{Total Debt}}{\text{Total Assets}}$$

or alternatively:

$$\text{Debt ratio} = \frac{\text{Total Liability}}{\text{Total Assets}}$$

For example, a company with $2 million in total assets and $500,000 in total liabilities would have a _____ of 25%

Like all financial ratios, a company's _____ should be compared with their industry average or other competing firms.

   a. Profitability index
   b. 3M Company
   c. Finance lease
   d. Debt ratio

36. In finance, a _____ or accounting ratio is a ratio of two selected numerical values taken from an enterprise's financial statements. There are many standard ratios used to try to evaluate the overall financial condition of a corporation or other organization. _____s may be used by managers within a firm, by current and potential shareholders (owners) of a firm, and by a firm's creditors.
   a. Current ratio
   b. Financial ratio
   c. Price/cash flow ratio
   d. Return of capital

37. _____ or interest coverage ratio is a measure of a company's ability to honor its debt payments. It may be calculated as either EBIT or EBITDA divided by the total interest payable.

   a. Capital recovery factor
   b. Yield Gap
   c. Return of capital
   d. Times interest earned

38. In accounting, _____ or carrying value is the value of an asset according to its balance sheet account balance. For assets, the value is based on the original cost of the asset less any depreciation, amortization or impairment costs made against the asset. Traditionally, a company's _____ is its total assets minus intangible assets and liabilities.
   a. Depreciation
   b. Generally accepted accounting principles
   c. Book value
   d. Matching principle

Chapter 12. Equity Financing

1. A _____ is a type of debt Like all debt instruments, a _____ entails the redistribution of financial assets over time, between the lender and the borrower.
    a. Lender
    b. Loan to value
    c. Loan
    d. Debenture

2. _____ in accounting is the process of treating equity investments, usually 20-50%, in associate companies. The investor keeps such equities as an asset. Proportional share of associate company's net income increases the investment, and proportional payment of dividends decreases it.
    a. Out-of-pocket
    b. AIG
    c. ABC Television Network
    d. Equity method

3. A _____ is a fungible, negotiable instrument representing financial value. they are broadly categorized into debt securities (such as banknotes, bonds and debentures), and equity securities; e.g., common stocks. The company or other entity issuing the _____ is called the issuer.
    a. Security
    b. 3M Company
    c. BMC Software, Inc.
    d. Tracking stock

4. In financial accounting, a _____ is defined as an obligation of an entity arising from past transactions or events, the settlement of which may result in the transfer or use of assets, provision of services or other yielding of economic benefits in the future.
    a. False Claims Act
    b. Vested
    c. Liability
    d. Corporate governance

5. A _____ is a type of business entity in which partners (owners) share with each other the profits or losses of the business undertaking in which all have invested. _____s are often favored over corporations for taxation purposes, as the _____ structure does not generally incur a tax on profits before it is distributed to the partners (i.e. there is no dividend tax levied.) However, depending on the _____ structure and the jurisdiction in which it operates, owners of a _____ may be exposed to greater personal liability than they would as shareholders of a corporation.

a. Partnership
b. Resource Conservation and Recovery Act
c. Corporate governance
d. National Information Infrastructure Protection Act

6. A sole _____, or simply _____ is a type of business entity which legally has no separate existence from its owner. Hence, the limitations of liability enjoyed by a corporation and limited liability partnerships do not apply to sole proprietors. All debts of the business are debts of the owner.
   a. Pre-determined overhead rate
   b. Free cash flow
   c. Safety stock
   d. Proprietorship

7. In economics, _____ or _____ goods or real _____ refers to factors of production used to create goods or services that are not themselves significantly consumed (though they may depreciate) in the production process. _____ goods may be acquired with money or financial _____. In finance and accounting, _____ generally refers to financial wealth, especially that used to start or maintain a business.
   a. Screening
   b. Capital
   c. Vyborg Appeal
   d. Disclosure

8. _____ is the planning process used to determine whether a firm's long term investments such as new machinery, replacement machinery, new plants, new products, and research development projects are worth pursuing. It is budget for major capital, or investment, expenditures.

Many formal methods are used in _____, including the techniques such as

- Net present value
- Profitability index
- Internal rate of return
- Modified Internal Rate of Return
- Equivalent annuity

These methods use the incremental cash flows from each potential investment, or project. Techniques based on accounting earnings and accounting rules are sometimes used - though economists consider this to be improper - such as the accounting rate of return, and 'return on investment.' Simplified and hybrid methods are used as well, such as payback period and discounted payback period.

a. Gross profit
b. Capital budgeting
c. Cash flow
d. Preferred stock

9. _____ is a concept whereby a person's financial liability is limited to a fixed sum, most commonly the value of a person's investment in a company or partnership with _____. A shareholder in a limited company is not personally liable for any of the debts of the company, other than for the value of his investment in that company. The same is true for the members of a _____ partnership and the limited partners in a limited partnership.

a. Due diligence
b. Joint venture
c. Limited liability
d. Burden of proof

10. _____ is the state or fact of exclusive rights and control over property, which may be an object, land/real estate or intellectual property. An _____ right is also referred to as title.

_____ is the key building block in the development of the capitalist socio-economic system.

a. Ownership
b. Administrative proceeding
c. ABC Television Network
d. Encumbrance

11. The _____ are the primary rules governing the management of a corporation in the United States and Canada, and are filed with a state or other regulatory agency. The equivalent in the United Kingdom and various other countries is Articles of Association.

A corporation's _____ generally provide information such as:

- The corporation's name, which has to be unique from any other corporation in that jurisdiction. As part of the corporation's name, certain words such as 'incorporated', 'limited', 'corporation', (or their abbreviations) or some equivalent term in countries whose language is not English, are usually required as part of the name as a 'flag' to indicate to persons doing business with the organization that it is a corporation as opposed to an individual or partnership (with unlimited liability.) In some cases, certain types of names are prohibited except by special permission, such as words implying the corporation is a government agency or has powers to act in ways it is not otherwise allowed.
- The name of the person(s) organizing the corporation (usually members of the board of directors.)
- Whether the corporation is a stock corporation or a non-stock corporation.
- Whether the corporation's existence is permanent or limited for a specific period of time. Generally the rule is that a corporation existence is forever, or until (1) it stops paying the yearly corporate renewal fees or otherwise fails to do something required to continue its existence such as file certain paperwork each year; or (2) it files a request to 'wind up and dissolve.'
- In some cases, a corporation must state the purposes for which it is formed. Some jurisdictions permit a general statement such as 'any lawful purpose' but some require explicit specifications.
- If a non-stock corporation, whether it is for profit or non-profit. However, some jurisdictions differentiate by 'for profit' or 'non profit' and some by 'stock or non-stock'.
- In the United States, if a corporation is to be organized as a non-profit, to be recognized as such by the Internal Revenue Service, such as for eligibility for tax exemption, certain specific wording must be included stating no part of the assets of the corporation are to benefit the members.
- If a stock corporation, the number of shares the corporation is authorized to issue, or the maximum amount in a specific currency of stock that may be issued, e.g. a maximum of $25,000.
- The number and names of the corporation's initial Board of Directors (though this is optional in most cases.)
- The initial director(s) of the corporation (in some cases the incorporator or the registered agent must be a director, if not an attorney or another corporation.)
- The location of the corporation's 'registered office' - the location at which legal papers can be served to the corporation if necessary. Some states further require the designation of a Registered Agent: a person to whom such papers could be delivered.

Most states permit a corporation to be formed by one person; in some cases (such as non-profit corporations) it may require three or five or more. This change has come about as a result of Delaware liberalizing its corporation rules to allow corporations to be formed by one person, and states not wanting to lose corporate charters to Delaware had to revise their rules as a result.

a. Employee Retirement Income Security Act
b. Express warranty
c. Articles of incorporation
d. Exclusive right

Chapter 12. Equity Financing

12. A _____ is a body of elected or appointed members who jointly oversee the activities of a company or organization. The body sometimes has a different name, such as board of trustees, board of governors, board of managers, or executive board. It is often simply referred to as 'the board.'

A board's activities are determined by the powers, duties, and responsibilities delegated to it or conferred on it by an authority outside itself.

   a. Board of directors
   b. Hospital Survey and Construction Act
   c. Consumer protection laws
   d. Chief Financial Officers Act of 1990

13. A _____ is the grant of authority or rights, stating that the granter formally recognizes the prerogative of the recipient to exercise the rights specified. It is implicit that the granter retains superiority (or sovereignty), and that the recipient admits a limited (or inferior) status within the relationship, and it is within that sense that _____s were historically granted, and that sense is retained in modern usage of the term. Also, _____ can simply be a document giving royal permission to start a colony.
   a. Scottish Poor Laws
   b. False Claims Act
   c. Covenant
   d. Charter

14. _____ is a form of corporation equity ownership represented in the securities. It is a stock whose dividends are based on market fluctuations. It is dangerous in comparison to preferred shares and some other investment options, in that in the event of bankruptcy, _____ investors receive their funds after preferred stock holders, bondholders, creditors, etc. On the other hand, common shares on average perform better than preferred shares or bonds over time.
   a. Stock split
   b. Common stock
   c. 3M Company
   d. Growth investing

15. _____ is the imposition of two or more taxes on the same income (in the case of income taxes), asset (in the case of capital taxes), or financial transaction (in the case of sales taxes.) It refers to two distinct situations:

   - taxation of dividend income without relief or credit for taxes paid by the company paying the dividend on the income from which the dividend is paid. This arises in the so-called 'classical' system of corporate taxation, used in the United States.
   - taxation by two or more countries of the same income, asset or transaction, for example income paid by an entity of one country to a resident of a different country. The double liability is often mitigated by tax treaties between countries.

Chapter 12. Equity Financing

It is not unusual for a business or individual who is resident in one country to make a taxable gain (earnings, profits) in another. This person may find that he is obliged by domestic laws to pay tax on that gain locally and pay again in the country in which the gain was made. Since this is inequitable, many nations make bilateral _____ agreements with each other.

   a. Federal Unemployment Tax Act
   b. Tax shelter
   c. Carbon tax
   d. Double taxation

16. _____, also referred to simply as a 'public offering' or 'flotation,' is when a company issues common stock or shares to the public for the first time. They are often issued by smaller, younger companies seeking capital to expand, but can also be done by large privately-owned companies looking to become publicly traded.

In an _____ the issuer may obtain the assistance of an underwriting firm, which helps it determine what type of security to issue (common or preferred), best offering price and time to bring it to market.

   a. AT'T Wireless Services, Inc.
   b. Insolvency
   c. Intergenerational equity
   d. Initial public offering

17. A mutual shareholder or _____ is an individual or company (including a corporation) that legally owns one or more shares of stock in a joint stock company. A company's shareholders collectively own that company. Thus, the typical goal of such companies is to enhance shareholder value.
   a. 3M Company
   b. Stockholder
   c. Stock split
   d. Growth investing

18. Initial _____, also referred to simply as a '_____' or 'flotation,' is when a company issues common stock or shares to the public for the first time. They are often issued by smaller, younger companies seeking capital to expand, but can also be done by large privately-owned companies looking to become publicly traded.

In an Ipublic offering the issuer may obtain the assistance of an underwriting firm, which helps it determine what type of security to issue (common or preferred), best offering price and time to bring it to market.

Chapter 12. Equity Financing

a. Public offering
b. Gross income
c. Restricted stock
d. Commercial paper

19. _____ is typically a 'higher ranking' stock than voting shares, and its terms are negotiated between the corporation and the investor.

_____ usually carries no voting rights, but may carry superior priority over common stock in the payment of dividends and upon liquidation. _____ may carry a dividend that is paid out prior to any dividends being paid to common stock holders.

a. Restricted stock
b. Cash flow
c. Gross income
d. Preferred stock

20. In finance, a _____ is a type of bond that can be converted into shares of stock in the issuing company, usually at some pre-announced ratio. It is a hybrid security with debt- and equity-like features. Although it typically has a low coupon rate, the holder is compensated with the ability to convert the bond to common stock, usually at a substantial discount to the stock's market value.

a. Zero-coupon bond
b. Coupon rate
c. Zero-coupon
d. Convertible bond

21. A _____ is any one of a variety of different systems, institutions, procedures, social relations and infrastructures whereby persons trade, and goods and services are exchanged, forming part of the economy. It is an arrangement that allows buyers and sellers to exchange things. _____s vary in size, range, geographic scale, location, types and variety of human communities, as well as the types of goods and services traded.

a. Market Failure
b. Market
c. Recession
d. Perfect competition

22. _____, in finance and accounting, means stated value or face value. From this comes the expressions at par (at the _____), over par (over _____) and under par (under _____).

_____ is a nominal value of a security which is determined by an issuer company at a minimum price. _____ of an equity (a stock) is a somewhat archaic concept. The _____ of a stock was the share price upon initial offering; the issuing company promised not to issue further shares below _____, so investors could be confident that no one else was receiving a more favorable issue price. This was far more important in unregulated equity markets than in the regulated markets that exist today.

   a. Net worth
   b. Par value
   c. Restructuring
   d. Creditor

23. A _____ or reacquired stock is stock which is bought back by the issuing company, reducing the amount of outstanding stock on the open market ('open market' including insiders' holdings).

Stock repurchases are often used as a tax-efficient method to put cash into shareholders' hands, rather than pay dividends. Sometimes, companies do this when they feel that their stock is undervalued on the open market.

   a. Treasury stock
   b. Cost of goods sold
   c. Matching principle
   d. Net profit

24. In financial accounting, a _____ or statement of financial position is a summary of a person's or organization's balances. Assets, liabilities and ownership equity are listed as of a specific date, such as the end of its financial year. A _____ is often described as a snapshot of a company's financial condition.
   a. 3M Company
   b. Statement of retained earnings
   c. Financial statements
   d. Balance sheet

25. _____ are payments made by a corporation to its shareholder members. It is the portion of corporate profits paid out to stockholders. When a corporation earns a profit or surplus, that money can be put to two uses: it can either be re-invested in the business (called retained earnings), or it can be paid to the shareholders as a dividend.
   a. Dividend payout ratio
   b. Dividend stripping
   c. Dividend yield
   d. Dividends

Chapter 12. Equity Financing

26. _____ is a specific term used in companies' financial reporting from the company-whole point of view. Because that use excludes the effects of changing ownership interest, an economic measure of _____ is necessary for financial analysis from the shareholders' point of view

_____ is defined by the Financial Accounting Standards Board, or FASB, as 'the change in equity [net assets] of a business enterprise during a period from transactions and other events and circumstances from nonowner sources. It includes all changes in equity during a period except those resulting from investments by owners and distributions to owners.'

_____ is the sum of net income and other items that must bypass the income statement because they have not been realized, including items like an unrealized holding gain or loss from available for sale securities and foreign currency translation gains or losses.

   a. Comprehensive income
   b. BMC Software, Inc.
   c. BNSF Railway
   d. 3M Company

27. A _____ is the transfer of wealth from one party (such as a person or company) to another. A _____ is usually made in exchange for the provision of goods, services or both, or to fulfill a legal obligation.

The simplest and oldest form of _____ is barter, the exchange of one good or service for another.

   a. 3M Company
   b. Payee
   c. BMC Software, Inc.
   d. Payment

28. _____ is a legal term for a type of debt which is overdue after missing an expected payment. It is also used (in the form in _____) for payments that occur at the end of a period.

_____ accrue from the date on the first missed payment was due. The term is often used to describe being late with rent, bills, royalties (or other contractual payments), child support, or other legal financial obligation.

   a. Arrears
   b. Interest
   c. AIG
   d. ABC Television Network

29. _____ is the fraction of net income a firm pays to its stockholders in dividends:

The part of the earnings not paid to investors is left for investment to provide for future earnings growth. Investors seeking high current income and limited capital growth prefer companies with high _____. However investors seeking capital growth may prefer lower payout ratio because capital gains are taxed at a lower rate.

   a. Dividend yield
   b. Dividends
   c. Dividend stripping
   d. Dividend payout ratio

30. The general definition of an _____ is an evaluation of a person, organization, system, process, project or product. _____s are performed to ascertain the validity and reliability of information; also to provide an assessment of a system's internal control. The goal of an _____ is to express an opinion on the person/organization/system (etc) in question, under evaluation based on work done on a test basis.
   a. Audit regime
   b. Assurance service
   c. Institute of Chartered Accountants of India
   d. Audit

31. _____ is a company's financial statement that indicates how the revenue is transformed into the net income The purpose of the _____ is to show managers and investors whether the company made or lost money during the period being reported.

The important thing to remember about an _____ is that it represents a period of time.

   a. ABC Television Network
   b. AMEX
   c. AIG
   d. Income statement

32. _____ is generally understood in financial circles as the point at which revenue is recognized, typically through a transaction which involves the exchange of an asset, product, or service for cash or its equivalents.

Chapter 12. Equity Financing

This approach gives the accounting division a strictly objective basis for changing the books. For example, a homeowner may believe that his house has grown in value during a strong market, or fallen in value during a weak market, but until the house is actually sold for a specific price to a specific buyer, the change in value can only be estimated and is considered unrealized.

   a. Total-factor productivity
   b. Merck ' Co., Inc.
   c. Realization
   d. Valuation

33. In monetary economics _____ can refer either to a particular _____, for example British Pounds or United States Dollars, or, to the coins and banknotes of a particular _____, which actually form only a small part of the monetary base of a nation's money supply. The other part of a nation's money supply consists of money deposited in banks (sometimes called deposit money), ownership of which can be transferred by means of checks (cheques in the United Kingdom and Australia) or other forms of money transfer such as credit and debit cards. Deposit money and _____ are 'money' in the sense that both are acceptable as a means of exchange, but money need not necessarily be '_____'.

   a. BMC Software, Inc.
   b. 3M Company
   c. BNSF Railway
   d. Currency

34. _____ is an American publishing and financial information firm.

The company was founded in 1882 by three reporters: Charles Dow, Edward Jones, and Charles Bergstresser. Like The New York Times and the Washington Post, the company was in recent years publicly traded but privately controlled.

   a. Professional association
   b. MicroStrategy
   c. Multinational corporation
   d. Dow Jones ' Company

35. A _____ or stock divide increases or decreases the number of shares in a public company. The price is adjusted such that the before and after market capitalization of the company remains the same and dilution does not occur. Options and warrants are included.

a. Stockholder
b. 3M Company
c. Growth investing
d. Stock split

36. The _____ is one of the basic financial statements as per Generally Accepted Accounting Principles, and it explains the changes in a company's retained earnings over the reporting period. It breaks down changes affecting the account, such as profits or losses from operations, dividends paid, and any other items charged or credited to retained earnings. A retained earnings statement is required by Generally Accepted Accounting Principles whenever comparative balance sheets and income statements are presented.
a. 3M Company
b. Notes to the financial statements
c. Financial statements
d. Statement of retained earnings

Chapter 13. Investments in Debt and Equity Securities

1. _____ in accounting is the process of treating equity investments, usually 20-50%, in associate companies. The investor keeps such equities as an asset. Proportional share of associate company's net income increases the investment, and proportional payment of dividends decreases it.
   a. AIG
   b. ABC Television Network
   c. Out-of-pocket
   d. Equity method

2. _____ is the balance of the amounts of cash being received and paid by a business during a defined period of time, sometimes tied to a specific project. Measurement of _____ can be used

   - to evaluate the state or performance of a business or project.
   - to determine problems with liquidity. Being profitable does not necessarily mean being liquid. A company can fail because of a shortage of cash, even while profitable.
   - to project rate of returns. The time of _____s into and out of projects are used as inputs to financial models such as internal rate of return, and net present value.
   - to examine income or growth of a business when it is believed that accrual accounting concepts do not represent economic realities. Alternately, _____ can be used to 'validate' the net income generated by accrual accounting.

   _____ as a generic term may be used differently depending on context, and certain _____ definitions may be adapted by analysts and users for their own uses. Common terms include operating _____ and free _____.

   a. Controlling interest
   b. Commercial paper
   c. Flow-through entity
   d. Cash flow

3. _____ is that which is owed; usually referencing assets owed, but the term can also cover moral obligations and other interactions not requiring money. In the case of assets, _____ is a means of using future purchasing power in the present before a summation has been earned. Some companies and corporations use _____ as a part of their overall corporate finance strategy.
   a. Lender
   b. Loan
   c. Debenture
   d. Debt

4. A _____ is a fungible, negotiable instrument representing financial value. they are broadly categorized into debt securities (such as banknotes, bonds and debentures), and equity securities; e.g., common stocks. The company or other entity issuing the _____ is called the issuer.

a. Tracking stock
b. BMC Software, Inc.
c. Security
d. 3M Company

5. _____ are financial statements that factor the holding company's subsidiaries into its aggregated accounting figure. It is a representation of how the holding company is doing as a group. The consolidated accounts should provide a true and fair view of the financial and operating conditions of the group.

   a. Committee on Accounting Procedure
   b. Replacement cost
   c. Redemption value
   d. Consolidated financial statements

6. In vector calculus, _____ is a vector differential operator represented by the nabla symbol: ∇.

_____ is a mathematical tool serving primarily as a convention for mathematical notation; it makes many equations easier to comprehend, write, and remember. Depending on the way _____ is applied, it can describe the gradient (slope), divergence (degree to which something converges or diverges) or curl (rotational motion at points in a fluid.)

   a. Del
   b. BNSF Railway
   c. 3M Company
   d. BMC Software, Inc.

7. _____ are formal records of a business' financial activities.

In British English, including United Kingdom company law, _____ are often referred to as accounts, although the term _____ is also used, particularly by accountants.

_____ provide an overview of a business' financial condition in both short and long term.

   a. 3M Company
   b. Notes to the financial statements
   c. Statement of retained earnings
   d. Financial statements

Chapter 13. Investments in Debt and Equity Securities

8. _____ means the giving out of information, either voluntarily or to be in compliance with legal regulations or workplace rules.

- In Computer security, full _____ means disclosing full information about vulnerabilities.
- In computing, _____ widget
- Journalism, full _____ refers to disclosing the interests of the writer which may bear on the subject being written about, for example, if the writer has worked with an interview subject in the past.

- In law:
    - The law of England and Wales, _____ refers to a process that may form part of legal proceedings, whereby parties inform to other parties the existence of any relevant documents that are, or have been, in their control. This compares with the process known as discovery in the course of legal proceedings in the United States.
    - In U.S. civil procedure (litigation rules for civil cases), _____ is a stage prior to trial. In civil cases, each party must disclose to the opposing party the following: names of witnesses which it may use to support its side, copies of documents (or mere description of these documents) in its control which it may use to support its side, computation of damages claimed, and certain insurance information. _____ is related to, but technically prior to, the discovery stage.
    - In Company law (known as 'corporate law' in the United States), _____ refers to giving out information about public or limited companies or their officers, which might be kept secret if the company was a private company or a partnership.

- In real property transactions, _____ refers to providing to a buyer information known to the seller or broker/agent concerning the condition or other aspects of real property that would affect the property's value or desirability. These rules regarding what information must be disclosed, and whether the information must be disclosed even if a buyer does not ask, vary from one jurisdiction to the next.

a. Trailing
b. Tax harmonisation
c. Disclosure
d. Controlled Foreign Corporations

9. A _____ is any one of a variety of different systems, institutions, procedures, social relations and infrastructures whereby persons trade, and goods and services are exchanged, forming part of the economy. It is an arrangement that allows buyers and sellers to exchange things. _____s vary in size, range, geographic scale, location, types and variety of human communities, as well as the types of goods and services traded.
a. Perfect competition
b. Market
c. Recession
d. Market Failure

10. The _____ is one of the basic financial statements as per Generally Accepted Accounting Principles, and it explains the changes in a company's retained earnings over the reporting period. It breaks down changes affecting the account, such as profits or losses from operations, dividends paid, and any other items charged or credited to retained earnings. A retained earnings statement is required by Generally Accepted Accounting Principles whenever comparative balance sheets and income statements are presented.
   a. Financial statements
   b. Notes to the financial statements
   c. 3M Company
   d. Statement of retained earnings

11. _____ is a specific term used in companies' financial reporting from the company-whole point of view. Because that use excludes the effects of changing ownership interest, an economic measure of _____ is necessary for financial analysis from the shareholders' point of view

_____ is defined by the Financial Accounting Standards Board, or FASB, as 'the change in equity [net assets] of a business enterprise during a period from transactions and other events and circumstances from nonowner sources. It includes all changes in equity during a period except those resulting from investments by owners and distributions to owners.'

_____ is the sum of net income and other items that must bypass the income statement because they have not been realized, including items like an unrealized holding gain or loss from available for sale securities and foreign currency translation gains or losses.

   a. 3M Company
   b. BNSF Railway
   c. Comprehensive income
   d. BMC Software, Inc.

12. _____ is generally understood in financial circles as the point at which revenue is recognized, typically through a transaction which involves the exchange of an asset, product, or service for cash or its equivalents.

This approach gives the accounting division a strictly objective basis for changing the books. For example, a homeowner may believe that his house has grown in value during a strong market, or fallen in value during a weak market, but until the house is actually sold for a specific price to a specific buyer, the change in value can only be estimated and is considered unrealized.

a. Total-factor productivity
b. Merck ' Co., Inc.
c. Valuation
d. Realization

13. A _____ is the pinnacle activity involved in selling products or services in return for money or other compensation. It is an act of completion of a commercial activity.

A _____ is completed by the seller, the owner of the goods.

a. Sale
b. Tertiary sector of economy
c. High yield stock
d. Maturity

14. In finance, a _____ is a debt security, in which the authorized issuer owes the holders a debt and, depending on the terms of the _____, is obliged to pay interest (the coupon) and/or to repay the principal at a later date, termed maturity. It is a formal contract to repay borrowed money with interest at fixed intervals.

Thus a _____ is like a loan: the issuer is the borrower, the _____ holder is the lender, and the coupon is the interest.

a. Zero-coupon bond
b. Revenue bonds
c. Coupon rate
d. Bond

15. _____ is a fee paid on borrowed assets. It is the price paid for the use of borrowed money , or, money earned by deposited funds .Assets that are sometimes lent with _____ include money, shares, consumer goods through hire purchase, major assets such as aircraft, and even entire factories in finance lease arrangements. The _____ is calculated upon the value of the assets in the same manner as upon money.

a. Insolvency
b. ABC Television Network
c. AIG
d. Interest

16. A _____ is a type of bond that allows the issuer of the bond to retain the privilege of redeeming the bond at some point before the bond reaches the date of maturity. In other words, on the call dates, the issuer has the right, but not the obligation, to buy back the bonds from the bond holders at the call price. Technically speaking, the bonds are not really bought and held by the issuer but cancelled immediately.

a. Coupon rate
b. Catastrophe bonds
c. Zero-coupon
d. Callable bond

17. Discounting is a financial mechanism in which a debtor obtains the right to delay payments to a creditor, for a defined period of time, in exchange for a charge or fee. Essentially, the party that owes money in the present purchases the right to delay the payment until some future date. The _____, or charge, is simply the difference between the original amount owed in the present and the amount that has to be paid in the future to settle the debt.

a. Discount
b. Discount factor
c. Risk aversion
d. Discounting

18. _____ is the process of increasing, or accounting for, an amount over a period of time. Particular instances of the term include:

- _____, the allocation of a lump sum amount to different time periods, particularly for loans and other forms of finance, including related interest or other finance charges.
    - _____ schedule, a table detailing each periodic payment on a loan (typically a mortgage), as generated by an _____ calculator.
    - Negative _____, an _____ schedule where the loan amount actually increases through not paying the full interest
- Amortized analysis, analyzing the execution cost of algorithms over a sequence of operations.
- _____ of capital expenditures of certain assets under accounting rules, particularly intangible assets, in a manner analogous to depreciation.
- _____

a. Annuity
b. Intangible
c. Amortization
d. EBIT

19. _____ is a life of security. It may also refer to the final payment date of a loan or other financial instrument, at which point all remaining interest and principal is due to be paid.

Chapter 13. Investments in Debt and Equity Securities

1, 3, 6 months _____ band can be calculated by using 30-day per month periods. For _____ bands over a year it is acceptable to use 365 day per year. For example with a Treasury Bond, its _____ is the date on which the principal is paid.

a. Factor
b. Statements of Financial Accounting Standards No. 133, Accounting for Derivative
Instruments and Hedging Activities
c. The Goodyear Tire ' Rubber Company
d. Maturity

20. _____ in business is an accounting concept that refers to ownership of a company (subsidiary) that is less than 50% of outstanding shares. _____ belongs to other investors and is reported on the consolidated balance sheet of the owning company to reflect the claim on assets belonging to other, non-controlling shareholders. Also, _____ is reported on the consolidated income statement as a share of profit belonging to minority shareholders.

a. Minority interest
b. Credit memo
c. Bankruptcy prediction
d. Subledger

Chapter 14. The Statement of Cash Flows

1. _____ is the balance of the amounts of cash being received and paid by a business during a defined period of time, sometimes tied to a specific project. Measurement of _____ can be used

   - to evaluate the state or performance of a business or project.
   - to determine problems with liquidity. Being profitable does not necessarily mean being liquid. A company can fail because of a shortage of cash, even while profitable.
   - to project rate of returns. The time of _____s into and out of projects are used as inputs to financial models such as internal rate of return, and net present value.
   - to examine income or growth of a business when it is believed that accrual accounting concepts do not represent economic realities. Alternately, _____ can be used to 'validate' the net income generated by accrual accounting.

   _____ as a generic term may be used differently depending on context, and certain _____ definitions may be adapted by analysts and users for their own uses. Common terms include operating _____ and free _____.

   a. Controlling interest
   b. Commercial paper
   c. Flow-through entity
   d. Cash flow

2. _____ is equal to the income that a firm has after subtracting costs and expenses from the total revenue. _____ can be distributed among holders of common stock as a dividend or held by the firm as retained earnings.

   The items deducted will typically include tax expense, financing expense (interest expense), and minority interest. Likewise, preferred stock dividends will be subtracted too, though they are not an expense.

   a. Long-term liabilities
   b. Generally accepted accounting principles
   c. Matching principle
   d. Net income

3. In financial accounting, a _____ or Statement of cash flows is a financial statement that shows a company's flow of cash. The money coming into the business is called cash inflow, and money going out from the business is called cash outflow. The statement shows how changes in balance sheet and income accounts affect cash and cash equivalents, and breaks the analysis down to operating, investing, and financing activities.
   a. BMC Software, Inc.
   b. BNSF Railway
   c. 3M Company
   d. Cash flow statement

4. _____ are the most liquid assets found within the asset portion of a company's balance sheet. Cash equivalents are assets that are readily convertible into cash, such as money market holdings, short-term government bonds or Treasury bills, marketable securities and commercial paper. _____ are distinguished from other investments through their short-term existence; they mature within 3 months whereas short-term investments are 12 months or less, and long-term investments are any investments that mature in excess of 12 months.

   a. Payback period
   b. Debtor
   c. Par value
   d. Cash and cash equivalents

5. _____ is the state or fact of exclusive rights and control over property, which may be an object, land/real estate or intellectual property. An _____ right is also referred to as title.

   _____ is the key building block in the development of the capitalist socio-economic system.

   a. Encumbrance
   b. ABC Television Network
   c. Ownership
   d. Administrative proceeding

6. In financial accounting, a _____ or statement of financial position is a summary of a person's or organization's balances. Assets, liabilities and ownership equity are listed as of a specific date, such as the end of its financial year. A _____ is often described as a snapshot of a company's financial condition.

   a. Statement of retained earnings
   b. Financial statements
   c. 3M Company
   d. Balance sheet

7. _____ is a company's financial statement that indicates how the revenue is transformed into the net income The purpose of the _____ is to show managers and investors whether the company made or lost money during the period being reported.

   The important thing to remember about an _____ is that it represents a period of time.

   a. AMEX
   b. ABC Television Network
   c. Income statement
   d. AIG

Chapter 14. The Statement of Cash Flows

8. _____ are formal records of a business' financial activities.

In British English, including United Kingdom company law, _____ are often referred to as accounts, although the term _____ is also used, particularly by accountants.

_____ provide an overview of a business' financial condition in both short and long term.

  a. Statement of retained earnings
  b. 3M Company
  c. Notes to the financial statements
  d. Financial statements

9. In vector calculus, _____ is a vector differential operator represented by the nabla symbol: ∇.

_____ is a mathematical tool serving primarily as a convention for mathematical notation; it makes many equations easier to comprehend, write, and remember. Depending on the way _____ is applied, it can describe the gradient (slope), divergence (degree to which something converges or diverges) or curl (rotational motion at points in a fluid.)

  a. Del
  b. 3M Company
  c. BNSF Railway
  d. BMC Software, Inc.

10. _____ of something is, in finance, the adding together of interest or different investments over a period of time such as atoms (1 - the act or process of accruing; 2 - the amount that accrues.) It holds specific meanings in accounting and payroll.

_____, in accounting, describes the accounting method known as _____ basis, whereby revenues and expenses are recognized when they are accrued, i.e. accumulated (earned or incurred), regardless when the actual cash is received or paid out.

  a. Earnings before interest, taxes, depreciation and amortization
  b. Accrual
  c. Accounts receivable
  d. Assets

ANSWER KEY

Chapter 1
1. c 2. d 3. d 4. a 5. b 6. a 7. c 8. a 9. c 10. d
11. b 12. a 13. d 14. d 15. d 16. b 17. c 18. b 19. d 20. d
21. d 22. a 23. d 24. a 25. d 26. a 27. b 28. d 29. b 30. c
31. a

Chapter 2
1. c 2. d 3. c 4. b 5. a 6. d 7. d 8. b 9. b 10. d
11. d 12. c 13. c 14. d 15. b 16. d 17. a 18. d 19. b 20. d
21. d 22. d 23. c 24. d 25. c 26. d 27. b 28. c 29. c 30. d
31. d 32. d 33. b 34. b 35. d 36. d 37. c 38. d 39. a 40. b
41. d 42. d 43. d 44. d 45. d 46. d

Chapter 3
1. d 2. a 3. d 4. a 5. c 6. d 7. a 8. a 9. a 10. d
11. a 12. d 13. c 14. d 15. a 16. d 17. b 18. d 19. d 20. c
21. d 22. c 23. d 24. a 25. d 26. c

Chapter 4
1. a 2. d 3. d 4. d 5. d 6. d 7. b 8. d 9. d 10. b
11. c 12. c 13. d 14. b 15. c 16. c 17. c 18. d 19. d 20. a
21. d 22. d 23. d 24. d 25. a 26. a 27. a 28. d

Chapter 5
1. a 2. d 3. d 4. a 5. b 6. a 7. a 8. d 9. b 10. d
11. a 12. d 13. c 14. d 15. b 16. d 17. c 18. d 19. b 20. d
21. d 22. d 23. d 24. c 25. a 26. c

Chapter 6
1. d 2. d 3. c 4. d 5. c 6. d 7. a 8. b 9. a 10. d
11. d 12. d 13. c 14. d 15. d 16. c 17. d 18. d 19. d 20. c
21. a 22. a 23. d 24. d 25. d 26. d 27. a 28. b 29. a 30. a
31. c 32. a 33. b 34. c 35. c

Chapter 7
1. b 2. c 3. c 4. a 5. a 6. d 7. a 8. c 9. d 10. d
11. d 12. c 13. d 14. d 15. c 16. d 17. a 18. d 19. d 20. d
21. a 22. a 23. a 24. c 25. a

Chapter 8
1. d 2. c 3. b 4. d 5. d 6. d 7. c 8. b 9. d 10. b
11. d 12. a 13. b 14. a 15. c 16. a 17. a 18. c 19. d 20. b
21. a 22. c 23. a 24. b 25. b 26. b 27. d 28. d 29. d

Chapter 9

1. c	2. a	3. c	4. d	5. c	6. c	7. c	8. d	9. c	10. d
11. b	12. c	13. d	14. d	15. c	16. d	17. c	18. d	19. c	20. b
21. d	22. d	23. d	24. a	25. a	26. d	27. a	28. a	29. d	

Chapter 10

1. a	2. d	3. d	4. a	5. d	6. a	7. a	8. d	9. d	10. d
11. a	12. d	13. c	14. d	15. c	16. d	17. c	18. a	19. d	20. d
21. d	22. a	23. b	24. d	25. d	26. d	27. a	28. d	29. d	30. d
31. d	32. a	33. d	34. d	35. a	36. c	37. d			

Chapter 11

1. b	2. a	3. a	4. d	5. d	6. d	7. d	8. b	9. d	10. a
11. d	12. b	13. d	14. a	15. d	16. d	17. c	18. d	19. a	20. d
21. d	22. a	23. d	24. b	25. d	26. d	27. d	28. d	29. b	30. b
31. c	32. d	33. d	34. c	35. d	36. b	37. d	38. c		

Chapter 12

1. c	2. d	3. a	4. c	5. a	6. d	7. b	8. b	9. c	10. a
11. c	12. a	13. d	14. b	15. d	16. d	17. b	18. a	19. d	20. d
21. b	22. b	23. a	24. d	25. d	26. a	27. d	28. a	29. d	30. d
31. d	32. c	33. d	34. d	35. d	36. d				

Chapter 13

1. d	2. d	3. d	4. c	5. d	6. a	7. d	8. c	9. b	10. d
11. c	12. d	13. a	14. d	15. d	16. d	17. a	18. c	19. d	20. a

Chapter 14

1. d	2. d	3. d	4. d	5. c	6. d	7. c	8. d	9. a	10. b

www.ingramcontent.com/pod-product-compliance
Lightning Source LLC
Chambersburg PA
CBHW082043230426
43670CB00016B/2763